Cultivating Faith
in fearful times

God bless you as you
grow in your faith!

Adele Blakey

Isaiah 26: 3-4,
41: 10

Cultivating Faith
in fearful times

Adele Blakey

Dedication

This book is dedicated with love to my husband, David. You have been an encouragement and a support to me throughout this writing project. Thank you for your confidence in me!

Contents

Introduction

How This Book Came to Be

My job as a software engineer left me emotionally and intellectually exhausted; I couldn't force myself to do much of anything else. The rational, analytical side of me had been engaged all day long while my artistic, creative nature was screaming for attention. Weekends were filled with miscellaneous activities that had been ignored during the week, such as paying bills, tidying up the house, and completing an entire week of Bible-study assignments. I was more frazzled on Saturdays and Sundays than during the week.

I let many things drop out of my life that had once given me much pleasure. As a young girl, I spent hours each day after school drawing houses, people, and portraits, or tirelessly singing and playing folksongs on my guitar. As a young adult, I still engaged in these activities and others, such as reading astronomy books and observing the night skies through my telescope.

As time passed the only activities I engaged in on a regular basis were Bible study and physical exercise. I longed to retire from the corporate world of work so I could once again enjoy the activities of my youth. I wanted so much to explore the creative person God had fashioned me to be.

More frustrating than a lack of time for artistic endeavors was my inconsistency in Bible study and prayer. These activities got pushed out to the last five minutes of my day when I was too sleepy to function. I was hungering and thirsting for God, but I didn't know how to exercise spiritual discipline when I felt so drained all the time. My faith wavered, and I struggled with guilt and self-condemnation.

Several of my friends prayed with me, and, after strong prompting, I met with a financial planner to see if I could make retirement a reality. His advice for me to wait two or three years depressed me, and I was very angry at God. Out of my anger I questioned God. He didn't answer me; however, He did wear down my stubbornness, and I was able to move on with my life.

A few months later my company decided to outsource a large portion of the software development jobs in my group. We were told that a small number of people would be laid off on March 31. The majority would be terminated in mid-December. Employees who wished to be considered for this reduction in force could apply.

While I felt bad for my fellow employees, a surge of excitement went through me. Based upon my length of employment with the company, if I were laid off in December my severance benefits would allow me to retire around the two-year time frame my financial planner had advised.

Many disconcerting questions permeated my mind. I was hesitant to move ahead of God and feared that volunteering for the layoffs would be an expression of faithlessness. I was attempting to fit God inside a box as I analyzed how He thinks and reasons. I didn't realize that my strong desire to be laid off in December inhibited me from sincerely seeking God's will for my life.

My husband agreed to leave the choice with me, so not believing I had heard anything from the Lord, I volunteered.

Three weeks later, I was told that my last day of work would be March 31st, not mid-December as I had planned. I was sick! What had I done? I would be unemployed nearly a year earlier than what my financial planner had advised, and my retirement pension would be less than what I had originally calculated. When I told my husband what had happened, his response was predictable: "You will just have to find another job." What ... was he crazy? Obviously he didn't understand! My technology skills were outdated, because for the past seven years I had worked on older systems, plus I hadn't interviewed for a job in more than 28 years. The more I ranted in my mind, the more panic-stricken I became.

I was convinced that I had acted rashly and was now suffering the consequences of my unbelief. Just when I thought my self-recriminations had reached their peak, I was told that the few employees who were being laid off in March were those who had volunteered. A more intense self-loathing settled in. What news could have been worse?

Days after the news hit, I was sitting in church, battling an onslaught of disparaging thoughts. I pulled tissue after tissue from my purse, blotting hopelessly at the tears. A friend wrote a short message on his bulletin and passed it to me. It read, "We are praying for you." I felt a flicker of hope as I allowed God's mercy to penetrate my self-absorbed anguish.

Friends and prayer comforted me greatly, but every time my thoughts shifted to the uncertainty of my future and the role I had played in losing my job, self-condemnation and dread would sweep over me. I had little defense against the fear, anxiety, and emotional paralysis that ensued. I knew Scripture implored me to "take captive every thought to make it obedient to Christ" (2 Corinthians 10:5), but I didn't know how to switch off these damaging thoughts whenever they invaded my mind.

Several years ago, I had memorized Psalm 139 and found it to be a wonderful, soul-engaging, spirit-lifting experience. Maybe what I needed was some strong, faith-based thinking that would engage my mind for an extended period of time, thus expelling the unwanted but firmly embedded thoughts.

Every conceivable emotion is expressed in Psalms, so I searched there first to find passages that called out to God for help in times of trouble. I have always been encouraged by the fact that even the most desperate Psalms contain an expression of hope and trust in

God, for no matter what the Psalmist was going through, he always conveyed the idea, "yet will I trust in Him!"

I reviewed the Psalms and many other comforting Scriptures that I had come to cherish over the years. Each morning, I would perch my Bible on the edge of the vanity and begin memorizing the few verses that I had just read. I would recite a small portion of Scripture until I felt confident that I could repeat it without peeking. On the drive to work, I would speak aloud the few verses that I had committed to memory. I kept a small Bible at work so I could verify my memory was still on track. I would play little games to challenge myself: while walking from my car to the building, I would try and recite the entire Psalm before I reached the door; when driving my car I would see if I could verbalize the relevant verses before I arrived at a certain intersection. Anytime my mind was not engaged in other mental activity, I would rehearse what I had memorized. I kept myself challenged by learning new Scripture as soon as I mastered the one I had been practicing. Before long I had a whole string of Psalms and other verses that I would recite one after the other as I allowed the rich meaning of the words to penetrate my mind.

In a few short weeks, I noticed something amazing. The fear, anxiety, and other troublesome thoughts had left me. I was starting to trust in God as never before. He had used Scripture to speak words of comfort and hope into my troubled soul.

That was when the idea for this book began. The wildly victorious results aroused in me a desire to encourage other Christians not only to grow but to flourish in their faith as they learn to trust God in all their circumstances.

With these thoughts in mind, it is my sincerest prayer that what I am going to share with you will help increase your level of trust in the Most High God, the Almighty One who is both willing and able to pull you out of your fear, anxiety, and unbelief no matter what your circumstances.

Chapter 1

Is Your Belief System Working for You?

…when the Son of Man comes, will he find faith on the earth?
(Luke 18:8)

My friend was driving on the freeway and was shocked to attention by a seven-foot metal ladder tumbling down the freeway like a twig. All the lanes of traffic were moving at full speed, and there was nowhere to go to avoid the ladder. In that split second all she could do was breathe the name of Jesus. The ladder hit the side of her car and ripped the rear tire to shreds. By God's grace she managed to get to the side of the road and call for assistance. That harrowing experience was the catalyst which drove my friend's faith to new heights!

Just how effective is your faith when it comes to handling the bumps and potholes of life? Do you fall apart when faced with challenges, or do you tighten your safety belt, shift your faith-gear into four-wheel drive, and hang on for one wild ride? Not every day of life will hold major challenges; how you handle the everyday stuff, however, is really the fruit of your faith life.

Regardless of your past experiences, the abundant life that Christ died to give you is not an elusive dream. You can experience the peace, joy, wholeness, and all-surpassing power the Scriptures assure us are ours in Christ during *this lifetime*. Spend some time alone with God and ask Him to help you. When you experience a sense of emptiness, depression, fear, anxiety, frustration, or other heart-sickening emotions, honestly confess those to Christ. He will not turn you away.

Difficult days are part of the reality of life, but the Bible clearly promises us that we can have personal victory every day of our lives. Troubles and grief will come; however, we can draw our strength from Him and weather the storms of life.

> *Therefore everyone who hears these words of mine and puts them into practice is like a wise man who built his house on the rock. The rain came down, the streams rose, and the winds blew and beat against that house; yet it did not fall, because it had its foundation on the rock. (Matthew 7:24-25)*

God has an intense desire for us to be effective and successful. He has called us to be victorious, and He wants us to prosper in whatever *He calls us to do*.

Read these New Testament verses promising victory and success to God's faithful:

- "So do not throw away your confidence; it will be richly rewarded. You need to persevere so that when you have done the will of God, you will receive what he has promised" (Hebrews 10:35-36).

- "I can do everything through him who gives me strength" (Philippians 4:13).

- "For God did not give us a spirit of timidity, but a spirit of power, of love and of self-discipline" (2 Timothy 1:7).

- "If you remain in me and my words remain in you, ask whatever you wish, and it will be given you. This is to my Father's glory, that you bear much fruit, showing yourselves to be my disciples" (John 15:7-8).

- "Let us not become weary in doing good, for at the proper time we will reap a harvest if we do not give up" (Galatians 6:9).

- "Now to him who is able to do immeasurably more than all we ask or imagine, according to his power that is at work within us" (Ephesians 3:20).

- "Being confident of this, that he who began a good work in you will carry it on to completion until the day of Christ Jesus" (Philippians 1:6).

- "No, in all these things we are more than conquerors through him who loved us" (Romans 8:37).

God's awe-inspiring promises are truly amazing! But what's more important is they are real and available to those who claim them and heed His warnings.

I have a few more questions:
- Do you believe God's promises?

- Do you believe in the One who made these vows?

- Do they bring you a calming sense of peace, hope, and assurance?

- Do they stir within you an exhilarating sensation of joy, excitement, enthusiasm, and courage?

- Do they give you the confidence to get out of bed every morning with determination?

Or maybe you are not quite so sure about them:

- Do you want to believe these promises but find it very difficult to do so?

- Do they depress you because you believe that they apply to only the "really great Christians" and not to you?

- Do some of these verses make you uneasy because you sense that they are calling you to make some kind of change in your life?

Perhaps they affect you in a very negative way:

- Do they make you angry because they don't measure up to your experiences?

- If they don't match up, does that mean these promises are fantasies—someone's delusional ideas of reality, maybe even outright lies?

- Do you believe that truth lies only within your experience, or is there a greater truth out there—one that just might be worth seeking?

Deep faith isn't something that just happens to you one day. You get there by cooperating with God's grace as you allow Him to nourish you on a *daily basis*. No matter how spiritually mature you are as a believer, God still calls each of us to dig deeper—and we can all use some encouragement to that end!

If you are skeptical or somewhere in between, I want to reassure you that I understand. I can recall a time in my life when I believed that God was unworthy of my trust. My pain was so intense and my disappointment so real that I turned my face from Him and simply walked away.

God loves you so very much, and He wants to call you into a deeper, more meaningful relationship with Him. There are many ways to get to know Him better. Being theologically well-informed gives you a basis for your relationship with Him. I hope you glean many excellent pieces of information from this book as we occasionally participate in an in-depth study of Scripture. You cannot trust in a God you do not know.

Intellectual discussions provide only one element in the pursuit of a relationship with God. The main purpose of this book is to encourage and motivate you toward the following goals:

- rise to the challenge that faith demands, especially in adverse circumstances; confidently believe that God will use your hardships as a means for spiritual growth and blessing.

- experience personal peace and reassurance by turning your fears and anxieties over to God.

- correctly understand God's promises and the conditions, if any, to which they are attached.

- understand the link between prosperity, fruitfulness, obedience, and trust.

- identify areas of distrust, patterns of disobedience, and recurring sin in your life and surrender those things to God.

- recognize that you were created and called by God for a glorious purpose.

- strengthen and personalize your faith so that it permeates every aspect of your life.

- gain control over your thought life and learn to effectively use the spiritual weapons that God has given to you as a believer.

- transfer your faith from your head to your heart.

As your faith in God grows, your level of stress will decrease along with your fears, frustrations, anxieties, and other negative factors in your life. This will have a very positive effect on your physical health.

I have grown very weary of spiritual ups and downs—the inconsistent spurts of genuine faith and obedience followed by unsettling bouts of disillusionment, frustration and discouragement; seeking God earnestly for a season only to find myself a short time later sewing fig leaves together and running off to hide in the bushes.

If you also feel exhausted by spiritual inconsistencies and conflicts, I invite you to come with me on a road trip. It will be bumpy, —full of protruding rocks and unexpected potholes. It will jar your bones at times, but every jolt of this thrilling ride will be worth it. And, please, do not be afraid, because God will be doing *all* the driving. I'm just His assistant tour guide; my role is simply to draw your attention to some points of interest along the way. So get in, fasten up your safety belt of truth, and come along with me on a thrilling ride!

I pray also that the eyes of your heart may be enlightened in order that you may know the hope to which he has called you, the riches of his glorious inheritance in the saints, and his incomparably great power for us who believe. (Ephesians 1:18-19)

The Logistics: How to Make the Most of This Book

The content of this book is designed for individual or group study.

I will encourage you along the way to make positive decisions involving your will. To cement a truth or enhance your ability to relate to the material being presented, I have included testimonies and life stories.

Understanding the Basics is aimed at laying a foundation of belief and trust in our Creator. First, we will examine what faith is and is not. Next, we will look briefly at what the Bible has to say and why we can trust it. Finally, we will take a look at our faith from God's perspective.

Growing Through Adversity acknowledges that life can be brutal at times, and most of us have experienced seasons in our lives when we felt let down by God. We need to understand "innocent suffering"—painful circumstances that were not brought about by our own foolishness or sin. In this section we will explore what the Bible teaches about adversity and what God may be trying to accomplish by allowing hardship in our lives. This section will also reveal the importance of responding to our difficult circumstances with integrity, faith and character. How we respond in our trials makes a huge difference—to God, to others, and to ourselves.

Prosperity, Obedience, and Fruit explores what the Bible has to say about these topics—how they relate and how faith is the key to all of them. This section also deals with difficulties in our lives that are brought about by our own sin or poor choices. Please do not let the subject of this section dishearten you, for you will find no words of condemnation in these chapters. God's Word boldly asserts: "Therefore, there is now no condemnation for those who are in Christ Jesus" (Romans 8:1). I hope to help motivate you to hunger for a more obedient lifestyle as you seek to overcome destructive behaviors that have become strongholds in your life.

Living Out Your Faith will help strengthen your faith as you learn how to take control over your thought life. We will investigate the mighty weapons God has given us to conquer our enemy. I will give you some practical ideas on how you can overcome destructive thoughts that have taken over your mind.

The closing pages of each chapter will contain the following common elements.

- A prayer designed to help you verbalize what you are learning and to assist you in connecting personally with God. He willingly delights in increasing our faith as we sincerely ask. Begin with the present measure of faith He has already given you. Included in Appendix C are lengthier prayers, each associated with a specific chapter. These prayers not only summarize what you have read, but they also help you communicate with God should you desire additional help in this area. *I strongly recommend that you begin each session by asking God to help you focus on the material. Ask Him to give you understanding and recall, and invite Him to show you how the material applies to your life.*

• Three sets of questions to help you down your road of faith. I hope you will take the time to answer them, because doing so will make our journey together more meaningful and ultimately rewarding. If you are honest with God and allow Him to have full access to your mind, emotions, and will, He will do an incredible work in your life.

If you are using this book as part of a group study, the first two sets of questions should be discussed among you, but only after each participant has read the specified chapter and answered the associated questions individually. Due to the personal nature of the third set of questions, they should not be discussed in your group.

Get It Straight is intended to stimulate your intellect and test your theological understanding of what you have just read.

Head to Heart is aimed at drawing your emotions and will into full play for a head-to-heart transfer.

You and God will help you connect with the information presented in the chapter on a very personal level. You will be asked to apply what you have read to specifics in your life. Since you are not going to be sharing these thoughts with others, I urge you to be as honest as possible with yourself and God.

• A relevant Scripture verse for you to memorize. This is a very powerful tool in helping you replace years of habitual negative thoughts and emotions with fresh, authoritative, faith-based thinking. Be sure to memorize the Scripture reference as well. There is nothing more frustrating than being unable to find your verse later.

• Several blank lines for your personal use. You may wish to note those concepts that touched you the most—little nuggets of wisdom and truth for you to savor. You may also use them to write a short prayer, a personal insight, a commitment, or a plan of action.

Throughout the book I included many Scripture passages in a format that is easy to relocate once you have finished this book. Some passages have been printed out for you to read. Others you will need to look up in your Bible. Please be diligent about reading them. God says that His Word will accomplish all that He desires. Do not minimize the power of that statement. Getting to know the Bible will have a profound effect on your life.

> *So is my word that goes out from my mouth:*
> *It will not return to me empty,*
> *but will accomplish what I desire*
> *and achieve the purpose for which I sent it.*
> *(Isaiah 55:11)*

All verses are from the New International Version (NIV) unless otherwise noted. At times I have emphasized words in a given passage through the use of ***bold italic print.*** I have done this simply to make a point; this emphasis does not appear in the actual NIV text.

I encourage you to read this book at a steady, consistent pace. Take time to let what you have read sink in, but don't lose your momentum by proceeding too slowly. My prayer is that the Holy Spirit will use what I have written to draw you closer to God as you live out your faith in everyday reality.

Prayer Time

Heavenly Father, thank You for the measure of faith that You have already given me. Open my heart and my mind; give me the courage to honestly and accurately assess where I am on this road of faith. Help me to be diligent. Reveal any inconsistencies in my life, especially things I claim to believe but don't put into practice. Please help me in my quest, for I know that I cannot accomplish it on my own. I pray this in Jesus' name. Amen.

Cultivating Your Garden of Faith

Get It Straight:

The following questions apply to each of the eight verses listed on pages 2 and 3. It will be helpful to look up these promises in the Bible and read them in their proper context.

1. What is the promise?

2. For what purpose is this promise given?

3. What conditions or warnings do you see associated with the promise?

4. Are any of the eight promises unconditional? If so, which one(s)?

Head to Heart:

1. Do you believe a person can experience joy and inner peace despite his or her circumstances? If so, how is this possible? If not, why not?

2. What do you hope to get out of this book? Which of the faith goals listed on page 5 are the most meaningful to you?

3. Think of a few events headlined in the news. Do you think God is sovereign over what is happening in today's world? Why or why not?

4. Do you have a favorite Bible verse? (If not, review the verses in this chapter.) Why is this verse meaningful to you? How does reading it make you feel?

You and God:

1. On a scale of 1 to 10, where would you place your level of faith?

2. How would you compare your level of faith to what it was a year ago?

3. On a scale of 1 to 10, how difficult are the circumstances of your life at present? What about one year ago?

4. Do you see a relationship between the level of faith you have now and the degree of pain or stress in your life?

5. Why do you think your faith has grown, diminished, or stayed the same?

Scripture Memory

Let us hold unswervingly to the hope we profess, for he who promised is faithful. (Hebrews 10:23)

Personal Thoughts:

_____

_____

_____

_____

_____

Chapter 2

What Is Faith?

He said to her, "Daughter, your faith has healed you.
Go in peace and be freed from your suffering."
(Mark 5:34)

Is the Christian faith rational, or must people reject reason in order to believe its tenets? Is it possible to truly believe in a God we cannot see? According to the Bible, what kind of faith is expected of Christ's followers?

A Functional Definition of Faith

Before I answer those questions, I have a confession to make. I love roller coasters! I also have two fun-loving girlfriends who share my enthusiasm for coasters. Every autumn the three of us drive to Southern California for our annual roller-coaster vacation. We systematically hit four parks in as many days, screaming our lungs out the entire time. Because most of the parks we visited last year had relatively short lines, we were able to ride more than eighty attractions. While a few were calm and kiddie-like, most of the rides were real white-knucklers. Although I love fast coasters and steep tracks, I am far from an adrenaline junkie. More than a few times, I've stood in line, silently praying, "Lord, this ride looks insane. If you don't want me on it, please knock some sense into me."

Have you ever ridden a roller coaster? If so, you understand the concept of faith. You pray that the coaster stays on the track and that the safety restraints keep you inside the car; you hope a mechanical failure doesn't occur and that you don't end up with a whiplash. Brilliant engineers designed the roller coaster; you are aware of the park's excellent safety record; you have watched many others ride the coaster without incident. Yet you don't know for a fact that you will get off that ride in one piece because the roller coaster has not yet finished its course. Only after safely exiting the coaster is your faith no longer needed—but only temporarily, for the minute you get back in line, the faith trip starts all over again.

Is roller coaster faith a stretch for your imagination? Let me assure you that similar faith is required every time you get into your car. Your safety is relying on the engineers who designed your car, the auto workers who built it, and the mechanics who maintain it, not to mention the faith you must have regarding the drivers you share the road with. You hope they are sober and alert, and you pray they are skilled drivers exercising good judgment when they get behind the wheel.

Faith is choosing to trust the roller coaster, the car brakes, or anything else you depend on throughout the day. Simply stated, faith is a decision to trust.

Most everything we do is based on faith. Take a few minutes and think about what your life would be like if you couldn't trust anything or anybody. For starters:

- You would never leave your house; in fact, you wouldn't live in a house, because the roof might collapse or you might be asphyxiated by a gas leak.

- You would never get into a car, a bus, a plane, a boat, or a train. You would never ride a bicycle, a horse, a snowmobile, or any other form of transportation. How do you know that it wouldn't run off the road, fall out of the sky, sink, explode, etc?

- You would never sit or lie down on anything, because it might collapse.

- You would never eat food that has been grown, processed, packaged, or prepared by someone else, since it may have been poisoned. In fact, you would not drink water, soda, coffee, or wine for the same reason.

I think I adequately made my case. If you had *no* faith you would be completely dysfunctional. In fact, you would probably be dead. Intelligent faith is based on logic, reason, and past experiences. It is a normal, healthy, desirable, and a necessary aspect of everyday life.

We have good reason to believe that a sturdy looking chair will hold us up, that the airplane will arrive safely at its destination, that we will not be poisoned by the medicine we picked up from the pharmacy. In spite of all the precautions we take, our faith in some things proves unjustified.

My nephew is a surveyor. He was conversing with a contractor beneath a newly constructed bridge, and less than a minute after they walked away, the bridge collapsed. Thank God no one was hurt! Were they foolish for standing under the bridge in the first place? Most people wouldn't think so. Why would anyone expect a new, sturdy-looking bridge to collapse on a calm, sunny day?

What Faith Is Not

How did the term *faith* get such a bad rap if *intelligent faith* is a part of daily life? Perhaps it is because most people have come to associate *faith* with *blind faith*.

Blind faith is not based on fact, evidence, reason, or experience. It simply decides to trust without attempting to investigate or verify that which has been postulated. Blind faith thrives on a lack of evidence. When proof is offered to the contrary, it is quickly discarded. The term describing this type of complacent acceptance should more accurately be called *blind ignorance* rather than *blind faith*.

We thrive on confidence and assurance, not doubt and insecurity. Most of us like to do a little research before we make major decisions or accept something as true. Evidence can be put into various groupings such as scientific, historical, spiritual, and sensory. Unfortunately, our postmodern culture tends to put *faith* in a realm where evidence has no place. This is a complete misunderstanding of the nature of faith.

Is Christianity Rational?

Many people mistakenly believe that Christianity is based solely on blind faith. They view Christianity as being completely incompatible with science, history, logic, and plain old common sense. While we are called to be people of faith, we most certainly are not expected to check our brains at the door.

Even intelligent faith entails a certain amount of doubt; it also requires that one makes a conscious decision to set aside those doubts and commit to a set of beliefs that cannot be proven. While faith goes beyond reason, it does not go against it. It is impossible to prove conclusively the existence of the triune God; in fact, attempting to do so would undermine the role of faith, which God so highly values (Hebrews 11:6).

There is a huge difference between rational faith and blind ignorance. The Bible does not demand that Christians exercise blind faith toward God; on the contrary, it highly discourages adopting such a reckless attitude.

Observe a few of the many Scriptures that encourage using one's mind through reason to investigate its claims:

• Christ taught that the most important commandment is to "Love the Lord your God with all your heart and with all your soul and with all your mind and with all your strength" (Mark 12:30). God wants our intellect be a factor in our decision to love Him.

- The apostle Paul beseeched the church in Thessalonica to "Test everything. Hold on to the good" (1 Thessalonians 5:21).

- Luke shows high regard for the Bereans because they scrutinized the preaching they heard. "Now the Bereans were of more noble character than the Thessalonians, for they received the message with great eagerness and examined the Scriptures every day to see if what Paul said was true" (Acts 17:11).

- Paul's persuasive method of preaching always contained logic and reason, not blind demands: "As his custom was, Paul went into the synagogue, and on three Sabbath days he reasoned with them from the Scriptures, explaining and proving that the Christ had to suffer and rise from the dead"(Acts 17:2-3).

The Old Testament is full of admonitions to seek wisdom, knowledge, understanding, and truth. The book of Proverbs has many such examples:

For the LORD gives wisdom, and from his mouth come knowledge and understanding. … For wisdom will enter your heart, and knowledge will be pleasant to your soul. Discretion will protect you, and understanding will guard you. (Proverbs 2:6, 10-11)

I, wisdom, dwell together with prudence; I possess knowledge and discretion. …Counsel and sound judgment are mine; I have understanding and power. (Proverbs 8:12,14)

While no one can prove beyond all doubt that God exists and that the Bible is true, we can certainly establish that belief in God is rational. We can attest that the Christian faith is a plausible explanation in understanding who God is. The field of Christian theology devoted to "proving" the Christian faith is known as apologetics. The term *apologetic* comes from the Greek word *apologia,* which means *to offer a defense.* It refers to a reasoned statement or argument. Its purpose is to present a rational basis for the Christian faith and to defend the faith against objections. It also seeks to expose the perceived flaws that many have leveled against Christianity. Apologists base their defense of Christianity on historical research, archeological evidence, legal and philosophical arguments, scientific investigation, as well as a host of other respected disciplines.

The discipline of apologetics addresses many topics; the following are some of the questions apologists seek to answer:

- Does God exist?
- Is Christianity rational?
- Can we know the truth?
- Are the Scriptures really God's Word?
- Is the Bible that we have today reliable and accurate?
- Did Christ rise from the dead?
- Is Christ deity?
- Are miracles possible?
- Are science and Christianity hopelessly in conflict with each other?
- How can an omnipotent, loving God allow evil and suffering?
- Is Christianity unique among all other world religions?
- Is Jesus the only way to God?
- Is there life after death?
- Do heaven and hell exist?

I could teach a course on how *not* to witness with examples of all the blunders that I have made. One of my most memorable is an encounter I had with a co-worker named Sylvia. Through the years we had engaged in a few interesting discussions regarding our religious beliefs. She was quite the skeptic. As a former Army nurse in Vietnam,

Sylvia claimed that any belief she may have had in God was decimated after what she'd seen. I don't pretend to have the answers to human suffering or evil; however, I tried to present logical arguments as best as I could.

One day that all changed. She used the "B.F." words. While making her case, she expressed the idea that Christianity was nothing more than blind faith and that she was too logical to believe in that kind of stuff. She repeatedly emphasized that as a software engineer she based her thinking on logic and reason, not on fairy tales.

Her words deeply offended me. We were both software engineers; I had been gifted with a logical mind as well. After giving my heart over to Christ four years earlier, I spent many hours reading books on the subject of Christian apologetics. I needed to be sure that my newfound faith was based on something more than emotion and blind faith. I craved rational evidence to bolster my belief. God, true to His Word, satisfied my hunger many times over.

So there I sat, stunned at what I was hearing and growing angrier by the moment. I had researched this; she had not. How dare she tell me that I was operating on blind faith! The only thing surpassing my anger at that moment was my pride. Both emotions overpowered me, and we soon got into an ugly argument. We made amends that afternoon, but I lost something valuable that day: the ability and opportunity to witness to her again.

The lessons to this story are legion, but the point I want to make is this: The belief that Christians operate out of blind faith is prevalent in our culture, and you will encounter it often if you discuss issues of faith with others.

In the next chapter I include some rational arguments as I defend the reliability of the Bible, but apologetics, for the most part, is beyond the scope of this book. For this reason, I have included a helpful bibliography on this subject in Appendix A.

I urge you to read apologetic literature for two reasons. First, it will strengthen your faith as it did mine. If you acquired your Christian beliefs from your parents and you have no idea why you believe the way you do, your faith will crumble. It might happen in college, or it may occur during a crisis, but it will happen. Paul Little, the author of *Know Why You Believe,* states it this way:

> If we know Jesus lives only because, as the hymn says, "he lives within my heart," we're going to be in trouble the first time we don't feel he's there. And when someone from a non-Christian position claims to have experienced the same thing from his god, our mouths will be stopped. We may choose to ignore doubts, but eventually they will "get to us." We cannot drive ourselves indefinitely by willpower to believe something of which we are not intellectually convinced. In fact, when someone tells us the only reason we believe is because of our parents and our religious background, we must be able to show ourselves and others that what we believe is objectively true, regardless of who told us.[1]

Second, you need to defend your faith for the benefit of others. But please, not the way I did with Sylvia. Many non-Christians reject the Bible's claims because no one ever presented the facts to them in a persuasive, logical manner. When objecting to Christianity they simply pull out the blind faith card. Sylvia didn't believe that Jesus was a historical person. She had never researched the subject and therefore had no idea that references to Jesus and to the beliefs of the early Christians were contained in secular writings of that day. Of course, intellectual objections are often a cover for the real problems: moral issues and pride. Unregenerate people deeply resent the idea of having to answer to a holy God. Rejection of Christ in this case is not so much a matter of the mind but the will. These issues can't be dealt with until the intellectual objections have been addressed.

Skeptics Welcome!

Thomas was quite the skeptic. He had a logical, scientific mind that thrived on empirical evidence. This became evident after Christ's resurrection when Thomas refused to believe the other disciples had seen the risen Lord.

Then Jesus told him, "Because you have seen me, you have believed; blessed are those who have not seen and yet have believed" (John 20:29).

After his encounter with the risen Lord, Thomas went out into the world and boldly preached the gospel. He eventually died a martyr for his unshakable faith.

Although Jesus gives a special blessing to those who believe without seeing, He was not offended by Thomas's skepticism, nor is He offended by honest doubts or difficult questions you may have. God is against passive indifference and stubborn, resistant unbelief. Come to Him with a sincere and open heart, and He will make himself known to you. Examine the Scriptures, read books that defend the faith, and seek God in prayer. The following is God's promise to you: "You will seek me and find me when you seek me with all your heart" (Jeremiah 29:13).

Biblical Faith Defined

Let's go a little deeper now and discuss more fully the kind of faith that God is looking for.

The Greek word for *faith* is the noun *pistis*. Other equivalent English words for *pistis* are trust or confidence in; belief; faithfulness, as in the character of one who can be relied on; fidelity.

In the New Testament, *pistis* denotes a conviction or belief regarding man's relationship to God and the things of God. It includes the idea of trust and holy fervor born of faith.

- relating to God: confidence that God exists and is the creator and ruler of all things, the provider and bestower of eternal salvation through Christ

- relating to Christ: a strong conviction that Jesus is the Messiah, through whom we obtain eternal salvation in the kingdom of God

Notice that the concept of trust and holy fervor is attached to the definition of faith. To the New Testament writers, true faith was never meant to consist solely of intellectual acknowledgement regarding the existence of God. Faith involved commitment. As the following verse indicates, even the demons intellectually know who God is, but they do not obey Him.

You believe that there is one God. Good! Even the demons believe that—and shudder. (James 2:19)

Observe in the following passages that faith is often used in the context of salvation.

*For it is by grace you have been saved, through **faith**—and this not from yourselves, it is the gift of God—not by works, so that no one can boast. (Ephesians 2:8-9)*

*For God so loved the world that he gave his one and only Son, that whoever **believes** in him shall not perish but have eternal life. (John 3:16)*

It is important to understand that the word *faith,* when used in the New Testament, is not always referring to "saving faith." Words such as *believe* and *faith* must be understood in context. Examine the following verse of Scripture:

Consider it pure joy, my brothers, whenever you face trials of many kinds, because you know that the testing of your faith develops

*perseverance. Perseverance must finish its work so that you may
be mature and complete, not lacking anything. (James 1:2-4)*

James is writing to Jewish Christians, whom he addresses as
his brothers. He is encouraging them to hold on to their faith during
times of adversity. The word *faith* as used here refers to an issue of
trust, not salvation. As Christians, we may find ourselves in situations
where our faith fails us, especially during a trial or a temptation.
Our salvation is not in question, but we may have missed an excellent
opportunity to develop perseverance and grow stronger in the Lord.

The other New Testament word for *faith* is *elpis* (noun), *elpizo*
(verb). While this word is sometimes translated into our English
word *faith,* it usually conveys the idea of an expectation or a hope,
a hope for something good to come about, the joyful confident
expectation of eternal salvation, having hope in the Author of hope.
Take a look at 2 Corinthians 1:10 for confirmation.

When used in the New Testament *pistis* and *elpis* have similar
meanings, as you can see below. The word *faith* in the first part of
this passage is translated from the Greek noun *pistis*, whereas *hope*
is translated from *elpis*.

*We continually remember before our God and Father your work
produced by **faith**, your labor prompted by love, and your endurance
inspired by **hope** in our Lord Jesus Christ. (1 Thessalonians 1:3)*

Scripture clearly affirms that faith and hope are intimately linked
together: "Now ***faith*** is being sure of what we ***hope*** for and certain
of what we do not see" (Hebrews 11:1).

Faith, therefore, is a confident expectation that God will
accomplish all that He has promised us in Christ. This belief is so
strong, so vivid, and so real that it gives our souls a glimpse of what is
to come as though it were a present reality. In the mind's eye, we see
the truth of those things that we cannot discern with our physical eyes.
Faith is to the soul everything that our five-senses are to the body.

The close relationship between faith and hope makes the truth expressed in this Proverb very pertinent to our subject on faith:

Hope deferred makes the heart sick, but a longing fulfilled is a tree of life. (Proverbs 13:12)

The apostle Paul complements this very truth by asserting:

And hope does not disappoint us, because God has poured out his love into our hearts by the Holy Spirit, whom he has given us. (Romans 5:5)

Hopelessness does indeed disappoint us, and hopelessness most assuredly makes the heart sick. Don't miss this important truth. If you are feeling discouraged, hopeless, and sick at heart; if you are disappointed in God, your circumstances, or life in general, then your lack of faith is the real culprit. I urge you to examine your belief system. Evaluate your level of faith and your willingness to trust in God and His Word. And as you do so, remember where deception and lies originate. Jesus said of Satan,

He was a murderer from the beginning, not holding to the truth, for there is no truth in him. When he lies, he speaks his native language, for he is a liar and the father of lies. (John 8:44)

In contrast, read what Jesus says about the truth:

*Jesus answered, "I am the way and the **truth** and the life. No one comes to the Father except through me." (John 14:6)*

*"Sanctify them by the **truth**; your word is **truth**." (John 17:17)*

*To the Jews who had believed him, Jesus said, "If you hold to my teaching, you are really my disciples. Then you will know the **truth**, and the **truth** will set you free." (John 8:31-32)*

Jesus claimed that He is truth, that God's Word (the Bible) is the truth, and that we will be set free by the truth.

God understands your fears and anxieties. He knows the hardships and heartaches you have suffered, and He cares deeply! We have more than just a kind, sympathetic God who wants to help. He is the great I AM, and there is nothing He cannot do on your behalf. All He requires is a willing heart that cries out to Him. Give Him the measure of faith that you currently have, be it weak or strong, and ask Him to multiply it for you.

As you read this book I will be praying for you: that God will take you to a place of faith where you have never been, a wonderful place of hope, a place of rest and peace, a place where you will find a deep sense of satisfaction and assurance in Christ.

Prayer Time

Dear Heavenly Father,
I come before You with a heart and mind that sincerely wants
to know you. I am grateful that you welcome my honest doubts
and difficult questions. As I take this faith journey, I ask that
you make yourself known to me in a very real way. Fill me
with your assurance and sweep away any destructive doubts
that dwell within me. Amen.

Cultivating Your Garden of Faith

Get It Straight:

1. What is the postmodern view of faith in general and Christianity in particular?

2. Why is the study of apologetics important?

3. How do faith and hope tie together?

4. What does the New Testament teach about faith, passion, and commitment?

Head to Heart:

1. Why is it important for you as a Christian to understand not only what you believe but the evidence upon which it is anchored?

2. Christianity is not based on blind faith. Is it possible for a Christian to operate out of blind faith? (Think about your answer to the preceding question as you consider this.)

3. Have you read any books on Christian apologetics? If so, did they help to cement your faith? Which ones would you recommend to others?

4. Do you have friends or family who think Christianity is little more than blind faith? Have you had discussions about Christianity with them? If so, what was their response? Take some time to pray for them right now.

5. If you were a little more versed in some of the apologetic issues do you think you would be more willing to have such discussions with others?

You and God:

The following questions apply to the apologetic concerns listed on page 20.

1. Can you think of a time when your faith was shattered or you felt discouraged, hopeless, and sick at heart? Do you think having a firmer grasp on any of these apologetic issues would have kept your faith better intact? Which ones?

2. Which of the above questions cause you the most trouble with your faith?

🌱

3. Which ones are you most certain about?

4. Do you think your faith would be stronger if you had greater assurance about any of these topics? Would you be willing to investigate these issues further?

Scripture Memory

But in your hearts set apart Christ as Lord. Always be prepared to give an answer to everyone who asks you to give the reason for the hope that you have. But do this with gentleness and respect, keeping a clear conscience, so that those who speak maliciously against your good behavior in Christ may be ashamed of their slander. (1 Peter 3:15-16)

Personal Thoughts:

Chapter 3

Can You Trust the Bible?

We did not follow cleverly invented stories when we told you
about the power and coming of our Lord Jesus Christ, but we
were eyewitnesses of his majesty. (2 Peter 1:16)

As an enthusiastic new Christian, I attended a Bible study
on the book of Genesis. During the class I became confused and
troubled by many questions. Where did all the people come from
in Genesis 4:14-17? If God is all-knowing, why (in Genesis 22) did
He test Abraham? Who were the sons of God and the daughters
of men in Genesis 6:1-2; were these verses implying that angels had
sexual relations with human women? My thoughts went back to
the fanciful stories of Greek mythology: Zeus appearing in human
form and seducing beautiful maidens. The covenant of the rainbow
in Genesis 9:12-17 also bothered me for the same reason; it seemed
mythological in nature. What was the Bible saying in these and
other passages? Was I being asked to believe in legends?

I began to wonder: Who wrote these stories; how did the author
acquire them; what were his sources? My sense of apprehension
deepened as I continued to read. Had I turned my life over to God

only to be conned into believing myths? I prayed fervently, asking God to help me find the answers. Over the next few months He led me to the apologetics aisle of my local Christian bookstore. There I found information that helped me work through my confusion and restore my faith.

An increasing number of people in our postmodern culture don't take the Bible seriously; they have real doubts about it being the "Word of God." Where do you stand on this issue? Do you believe that the *entire* Bible is the *inspired, inerrant* Word of God? Perhaps you consider it to be merely a collection of man's beliefs about a God that we can never know, or maybe you are somewhere in the middle, reasoning that the Bible contains a mixture of God's words and man's opinions. Why do you hold your particular view and how did you come to that conclusion?

What Claims Does the Bible Make?

Hold on to those thoughts because, I would like us to explore what the Bible has to say about itself as well as what Jesus Himself believed regarding the Scriptures.

Approximately 1,943 years ago the apostle Paul wrote:

All Scripture is God-breathed and is useful for teaching, rebuking, correcting and training in righteousness, so that the man of God may be thoroughly equipped for every good work. (2 Timothy 3:16-17)

The Greek word for *God-breathed* is *theopneustos*. It means "given or inspired by God." It comes from two words *theos,* which means "God," and *pneo,* which means "to breathe or to blow." Many versions translate this word as *inspired.* I'm emphasizing this because I don't want you to confuse the biblical meaning of this word with the way we typically use it today, for example: "The artist was

inspired by the beautiful sunset" or "Your example has inspired me
to persevere." The word *inspired* in the biblical sense is unique and
refers to the *words* that have been written, *not* to the *writers* themselves.
The Bible claims to be God's Words coming forth from His mouth,
divinely authoritative and completely inerrant.

> The Bible is the product of God himself. These are not
> mere human ideas, but God's divine character and will is
> revealed through these words. It is important to realize too
> that the writers of the Scripture were not mere writing
> machines. God did not punch them, like keys on a typewriter,
> to produce his message. He did not dictate the words, as
> the biblical view of inspiration has so often been caricatured.
> It is quite clear that each writer has a style of his own.
> Jeremiah does not write like Isaiah, and John does not write
> like Paul. God worked through the instrumentality of
> human personality, but so guided and controlled people
> that what they wrote is what he wanted written.[1]

Biblical inspiration also carries with it the concept of inerrancy.
According to Dr. Paul Feinberg:

> Inerrancy means that when all facts are known, the Scriptures
> in their original autograph and properly interpreted will
> be shown to be wholly true in everything that they affirm,
> whether that has to do with doctrine or morality or with
> the social, physical or life sciences.[2]

Additionally, notice the word *all* in the previous Scripture verse.
The Bible in its entirety was "breathed out by God." Every part had
its origins in God, not in man. The apostle Peter likewise says:

Above all, you must understand that no prophecy of Scripture came about by the prophet's own interpretation. For prophecy never had its origin in the will of man, but men spoke from God as they were carried along by the Holy Spirit. (2 Peter 1:20-21)

There are a multitude of examples where the Bible directly or indirectly claims divine inspiration.

- "Moses then wrote down everything the LORD had said" (Exodus 24:4).

- "This is what the sovereign LORD SAYS, ..." (Isaiah 7:7; 28:16; 49:22; 52:4).

- "The word of the LORD came to Ezekiel ..." (Ezekiel 1:3).

- "In the past God spoke to our forefathers through the prophets at many times and in various ways, but in these last days he has spoken to us by his Son" (Hebrews 1:1-2).

- "The revelation of Jesus Christ, which God gave him to show his servants what must soon take place. He made it known by sending his angel to his servant John" (Revelation 1:1).

The Bible makes other claims for itself.

- ETERNAL: Isaiah 40:8

- PERFECT: Psalm 12:6

- TRUSTWORTHY: Psalm 119:105

- TRUE: Psalm 119:43

- HOLY and RIGHTEOUS: Deuteronomy 4:8

The Bible extends divine inspiration to the New Testament writings and prophetic authority to John the Baptist (Matthew 11:7-15) and Jesus' disciples.

- Paul, writing to the church in Corinth, claimed prophetic authority. (1 Corinthians 14:37)

- Peter viewed Paul's writings as Scripture given from God. He declared them to be both prophetic and authoritative. (2 Peter 3:15-16)

- Paul quotes as Scripture a verse found in Luke's gospel. (1 Timothy 5:18; Luke 10:7)

- Paul claims the word preached to the Thessalonians is divine in origin. (1 Thessalonians 2:13)

What Did Jesus Say about the Bible?

Jesus regarded Scripture as the authoritative Word of God. He lived and died clinging to every word contained in the Holy Scriptures. This is dramatically brought out in two events. When He was tempted in the wilderness, Jesus shielded Himself against Satan's attacks by proclaiming three times "It is written …" (Matthew 4:4, 7, 10). On the cross, in great agony, Jesus quoted Scripture twice (Matthew 27:46, Luke 23:46). The following passages also demonstrate Jesus' attitude toward Scripture:

- Matthew 5:17-18

- Matthew 22:29

- Luke 24:25-27

- John 17:17

Additionally, we can see from Scripture that Jesus believed in the Genesis account of creation (Matthew 19:4-6), the historical accuracy of David's life (Matthew 12:3-4), the events of Jonah (Matthew 12:39-41), the story of Noah and the flood (Matthew 24:37-39; Luke 17:26-27), and the destruction of Sodom along with the demise of Lot's wife (Luke 17:28-29, 32).

Today, many believe that the Bible contains a mixture of God's thoughts and man's thoughts. If this is true, then obviously all of Jesus' teachings regarding the Scriptures were inserted by man. This leads us to ask a rather disconcerting question: Where else was Jesus misquoted? There are many comforting words of Christ that we eagerly cling to. If our faith breaks down on His biblical claims, can we trust *any of His teachings with certainty?*

Hours before His death, Jesus told Pilot:

You are right in saying I am a king. In fact, for this reason I was born, and for this I came into the world, to testify to the truth. Everyone on the side of truth listens to me. (John 18:37)

If we accept Jesus as our God and King, and if we believe that He is the "the way and the truth and the life" (John 14:6), it behooves us to accept His teachings regarding Scripture.

Other Evidence

None of what I have discussed *proves* that the Bible is the inspired Word of God, but it does show us that the Bible *claims* to be of divine origin.

In the remainder of this chapter I will examine biblical data from an objective point of view, briefly laying out some basic arguments for the Bible's reliability. We will consider how well the Bible has weathered the test of time and the scrutiny of history, archeology, and prophecy.

My objective is to show you that sound, rational evidence does exist. I hope this will pique your interest and challenge you to seek further information on your own. (See the apologetic bibliographies in Appendix A.) Whenever you study apologetic literature, be sure to weigh the evidence as a whole; none of the presented arguments are meant to stand by themselves.

The Continuity of the Bible

The Bible truly is an amazing book. It is unique in its continuity in spite of its great diversity. The Bible was written:

1. over a 1,500-year span

2. by more than forty authors from every walk of life: kings, military leaders, peasants, fishermen, tax collectors, scholars, peasants, musicians, etc.

3. on three continents: Asia, Africa, Europe

4. in different settings: wilderness, dungeons, prisons, palaces, in exile, while traveling, and so forth.

5. at different times: peace, prosperity, war, famine, etc.

6. in different moods: joy, despair, confusion, doubt, certainty, etc.

7. in three languages: Hebrew, Aramaic, Greek

8. in a wide variety of literary styles: poetry, historical narrative, song, romance, memoirs, law, prophecy, parables, instructions, etc.

9. on hundreds of controversial subjects[3]

In spite of the great variances, the Bible is amazingly consistent and harmonious. It has been written with a single unfolding story: God's redemption of humankind.

You will find there is a unity of thought that indicates that one Mind inspired the writing of the whole series of books, that it bears on its face the stamp of its Author, that it is in every sense the Word of God.[4]

Confirmation of the Bible through History

The Bible was written on perishable material such as papyrus and parchment. Until the printing press was invented, it was copied and recopied by hand. Since each testament has its own tradition, we must critique them separately.

The Old Testament

Unfortunately, we only have a few Hebrew Old Testament manuscripts that date from the tenth century A.D., for out of reverence for God's Word, the Jews ceremoniously buried all flawed and worn out copies. In spite of this, we can be confident that today's Old Testament is faithful to the original manuscripts.[5]

Credit must be given to the devout manner in which the Jews passed down the manuscripts. The task of transcribing the sacred scrolls was performed by pious Jews who had a profound reverence for the Scriptures, believing them to be the very words of God. For instance, each time the sacred name of God was written, the scribe had to perform an elaborate religious ritual. The scribes also took painstaking measures to ensure that the finished manuscript was identical to the original. Every letter, syllable, word, and paragraph was counted. If the numbers didn't add up correctly, the entire scroll was destroyed.[6]

The Old Testament Bibliographical Test

Regardless of who prepared them or where they were found (Palestine, Syria, Egypt), the copies agree to an amazing extent. In addition, they coincide with other ancient sources, such as the Septuagint (the Greek translation of the Old Testament), which dates from the second and third century B.C.[7]

In 1947 the Dead Sea Scrolls were found hidden inside ancient jars in caves. They were placed there by a communal society of Jews who lived in the region from about 150 B.C. to A.D. 70. This find included the earliest manuscript copy yet of the complete book of Isaiah along with fragments of almost every book in the Old Testament.[8]

Biblical scholar, author, and educator Gleason Archer stated:

> Even though the two copies of Isaiah discovered in Qumran Cave 1 near the Dead Sea in 1947 were a thousand years earlier than the oldest dated manuscript previously known (A.D. 980), they proved to be word for word identical with our standard Hebrew Bible in more than 95 percent of the text. The 5 percent of variation consisted chiefly of obvious slips of the pen and variations in spelling. They do not affect the message of revelation in the slightest.[9]

The New Testament

For the New Testament, the evidence is even more remarkable. There are 5,700 Greek manuscripts and manuscript portions in existence today. Some of the earliest date from the second century, only 30-plus years after they were originally written by the apostles and their associates!

Additionally, there are 10,000 copies of the Latin Vulgate and 9,300 manuscripts in other languages. This means that we have about 25,000 manuscript copies or portions of the New Testament in existence today. Add to those 36,000 quotations of the New Testament from the early church fathers (A.D. 100–300).[10]

When we compare this with other works of antiquity, the contrast is startling. Of sixteen well-known classical Greek authors, the typical number of copies still in existence today is less than ten. What's more, the earliest copies date from 750 to 1,600 years after they were first written.[11]

With the abundance of manuscripts and manuscript pieces, scholars have determined that the New Testament text is 99 percent reliable. This 1 percent adds up to about 400,000 textural variants among the manuscripts. While this appears to be a lot, 75 percent of them are spelling differences or nonsense errors. Twenty-four percent are word-order changes that in no way alter the meaning of the text. The next largest group (less than 1 percent) of textural variants is not viable because they did not originate in the earliest manuscripts. They were found in much later copies (twelfth and fourteenth century). The smallest group of variants is meaningful, but they do not cause us to question any of our Christian doctrine. Scholars are satisfied that they possess substantially the true text of the New Testament.[12]

> The deity of Christ is untouched by these viable variants, the virgin birth is untouched, the resurrection of Christ is untouched. Everything that the Bible teaches that is a cardinal truth, an essential truth, is found there in the manuscripts and is untouched by the variants.[13]

The Internal Evidence Test—New Testament

Another test given to prove the historical accuracy of ancient manuscripts is known as the internal evidence test. This test analyzes the ability or willingness of the writers to tell the truth. The following types of questions are applied to the text: Did the writers use primary sources? Does the text contradict itself? Is there anything in their writings that cause us to doubt their integrity?

Nowhere in any of the New Testament documents is there evidence of fraud or error. Instead, we see mention of careful eyewitness reporting (Luke 1:1-3; 2; 1 John 1:3; John 21:24; 2 Peter 1:16). Furthermore, the kinds of details they included strongly suggest that they were men of high moral standards.[14]

They willingly recorded their own faults and failures (Matthew 26:56, 69-75; Luke 9:46). They included statements that would be embarrassing and perhaps harmful to their cause. For example, women could not give testimony in a Jewish court of law because they were considered unreliable witnesses. Yet all four gospels record that women were the first ones to see and report Christ's resurrection (Matthew 28:1-10; Mark 16:1-11; Luke 24:1-11; John 20:1-18). This probably accounts for one of the reasons the disciples did not believe them (Mark, 16:10-11; Luke 24:9-11).

They recorded some of the most difficult statements that Jesus made (Matthew 5:43-48; John 6:41-71) as well as charges against Jesus by His enemies. For example, Jesus was called a blasphemer (Matthew 26:65) and a liar (John 7:47-48). They said He was insane and demon possessed (John 7:20; 8:48, 52; 10:20).

The allegations of error in the Bible are usually based on a failure to recognize basic principles of interpreting ancient literature, for example:

- Study the context of the passage.
- Interpret difficult passages in the light of clear ones.
- Just because a report is incomplete does not mean it is false.
- The New Testament citations of the Old Testament need not always be exact.
- The Bible uses non-technical, everyday language.
- The Bible may use both round numbers as well as exact numbers.
- The Bible uses different literary devices.
- Later revelation supersedes previous revelation.[15]

The External Evidence Test—New Testament

Historians also use the external evidence test to verify the reliability of a document. This test seeks historical material from other sources in order to corroborate or falsify the documents.

Christian sources:

The early external Christian sources came from writers, church leaders, teachers, and apologists, many of whom were disciples of the apostles. They authenticated the gospels in their writings, confirming that they were written by the apostles or their companions. They firmly believed Jesus to be the incarnate Son of God.

- Clement of Rome (A.D. 95): bishop of the church at Rome.

- Ignatius (A.D. 70–110): bishop of Antioch. Christian tradition identifies him as a disciple of Peter, Paul, and John.

- Quadratus: a disciple of the apostles and the bishop of Athens.

- Justin Martyr (A.D. 100–167).

- Polycarp (A.D. 70–156): a disciple of John and a bishop in the Church of Smyrna.

- Eusebius: a fourth century church historian who preserved many of the early documents.[16]

Non-Christian sources:

- Tacitus, first century Roman historian: He gives the account of the great fire of Rome and the persecution that ensued. In his writings he speaks of Christians, who took their name from "Christus," who suffered at the hands of Pontius Pilatus. He refers to "a most mischievous superstition" that broke out in Judea and later in Rome. This most likely refers to the resurrection of Jesus.

- Suetonius, chief secretary to Emperor Hadrian, who reigned from A.D. 117–138: He confirms the report in Acts 18:2 that Claudius commanded all Jews to leave Rome in A.D. 49.

- Josephus, Jewish historian (A.D. 37–100): He makes many statements that verify the historical nature of both the Old and

New Testaments. Josephus gives a brief description of Jesus and his mission. He also mentions James, the brother of Jesus, as well as John the Baptist.

• Thallus, historian (A.D. 52): He writes about the darkness described in the gospels (Matthew 27:45; Mark 15:33; Luke 23:44).

• Pliny the Younger, Roman author and administrator: In a letter to the Emperor Trajan in about A.D. 112, he describes early Christian worship practices. He provides solid evidence that Jesus was worshipped as God and that his followers practiced the tradition of breaking bread together.

• Emperor Trajan: In reply to Pliny's letter he gives guidelines for punishing Christians.

• The Talmud, ancient Jewish writings: "Yeshu" was hanged on the eve of Passover.

• Lucian, second century Greek writer: His works contain sarcastic critiques of Christianity.[17]

Archeological Evidence

Archeology helped confirm many biblical accounts of events, places, and people. Norman Geisler and Ron Brooks, in their book *When Skeptics Ask,* have written:

In every period of Old Testament history, we find that there is good evidence from archeology that the Scriptures are accurate. ...While many have doubted the accuracy of the Bible, time and continued research have consistently demonstrated that the Word of God is better informed than its critics. ...

After the period of the Judges, the archeological evidence becomes increasingly clear that the biblical authors know what they were talking about. By the time we reach the New Testament period, the evidence for its historical reliability becomes overwhelming. ...

It was once thought that Luke had concocted his narrative from the ramblings of his imagination, because he ascribed odd titles to authorities and mentioned governors that no one knew. The evidence now points in exactly the opposite direction.[18]

For example, in his gospel, Luke makes a reference to "Lysanias, tetrarch of Abilene" (Luke 3:1). This man was unknown until an inscription mentioning his name and title was found recorded on a temple dedication. It is dated between A.D. 14 and 29, which is compatible with the beginning of John the Baptist's ministry.[19]

Scottish archeologist and New Testament scholar Sir William Mitchell Ramsay concluded after thirty years of study that "Luke is a historian of the first rank; not merely are his statements of fact trustworthy, ... this author should be placed along with the very greatest of historians."[20]

Through their archeological work, three of the greatest American archaeologists of the twentieth century—W.F. Albright, Nelson Glueck, and George Ernest Wright—radically changed their viewpoints regarding the Bible. All three men were trained in liberal scholarship, which took a dim view of the Bible.[21]

In later years W. F. Albright stated "There can be no doubt that archeology has confirmed the substantial historicity of Old Testament tradition."[22]

Likewise, biblical archeologist Nelson Glueck made the following statement:

It may be clearly stated categorically that no archeological discovery has ever controverted a single biblical reference. Scores of archeological findings have been made which confirm in clear outline or exact detail historical statements in the Bible.[23]

Prophetic Evidence

The fulfillment of biblical prophecies only adds to the reliability of the other information presented in the Old and New Testaments. In addition to the messianic prophecies the Bible contains many prophecies regarding the fate of certain cities and nations.

About 700 years B.C., God, speaking through the prophet Isaiah, told the nation of Israel that His prophetic revelations would prove that He alone is the one true God (Isaiah 44:7-8).

"Prophecy makes up a substantial portion of the Bible. There are over 600 direct references in the Bible to prophecy and prophets. Approximately 27 percent of the entire Bible contains prophetic material, much of which has already come true. Only four of the 66 books of the Bible lack any prophecies."[24]

Authors John Ankerberg and Dillon Burroughs in their book *Taking a Stand for the Bible* write of the late Peter Stoner, who was professor emeritus of science at Westmont College. Stoner, using the modern science of probability, calculated the probability of one man fulfilling eight of the major prophecies made concerning the Messiah. Stoner published the results in his book, *Science Speaks*. Stoner's work clearly showed that coincidence is ruled out by the science of probability. After examining these prophecies the conservative estimate of the probability of one man fulfilling these prophesies came to one in ten to the seventeenth power. (That's a one followed by seventeen zeros.) Stoner gave the following illustration to demonstrate how large this number is:

Imagine covering the entire state of Texas with silver dollars to a level of two feet deep. The total number of silver dollars needed to cover the whole state is $10^{17.}$ Now choose just one silver dollar, mark it, and drop it from an airplane flying over the state. Then thoroughly stir all the silver dollars all over the state.

When that has been done, blindfold one person, and tell him he can travel wherever he wishes in the state of Texas in an attempt to reach down into all those silver dollars and pull up the one that was marked. The chance of his finding that one silver dollar—in the entire state of Texas—would be the same as the chance the Old Testament prophets had for eight of their prophecies coming true about any one man in the future.[25]

In another calculation, Stoner used 48 prophecies (even though he could have used 456) and determined the chance that any one man fulfilled all of them was one in ten to the one hundred fifty-seventh power.[26]

The following table is a small sampling of Jesus' fulfillment of Messianic prophecies:

Prophecy	OT Prediction	NT Fulfillment
Of the house of David	Jeremiah 23:5; Isaiah 9:7	Matthew 1:1; Luke 3:31-32
Born of a virgin	Isaiah 7:14	Matthew 1:18, 22-25; Luke 1:26-35
Born in Bethlehem	Micah 5:2	Matthew 2:1; Luke 2:4-7
Heralded by the Lord's messenger	Isaiah 40:3; Malachi 3:1	Matthew 3:1-3
Would be mocked	Psalm 22:7-8; Isaiah 53	Matthew 27:29, 41-43
His hands and feet would be pierced	Psalm 22:16; Isaiah 53:5	Luke 23:33
His side would be pierced	Zechariah 12:10	John 19:34
Would be buried in a rich man's tomb	Isaiah 53:9	Matthew 27:57-60
Would rise from the dead	Psalm 16:10	Matthew 28:5-7; Acts 2:31
Would ascend into heaven	Psalm 68:18	Luke 24:50-51

What Is Your Verdict?

I hope you found this chapter to be "inspiring" as well as thought-provoking. The extraordinary measures taken to preserve the Holy Scriptures; the tests applied to the Bible (bibliographical, internal, external); and the testimony of history, archeology, and prophecy work together to confirm beyond reasonable doubt that the Bible is totally reliable. These findings are significant! Please take the time to study this further, especially if you are unconvinced.

The inerrancy and authorship of the Bible is highly controversial, and many denominations hold a more liberal view of the Bible. I do not wish to be deliberately offensive or argumentative, yet I am deeply concerned that the majority of people who hold a "man-made" view of the Bible have never investigated the overwhelming evidence that supports the Bible's claims of divine authorship. As we saw in a previous chapter, blind faith is an irrational faith, for there is either no evidence that exists or there is a refusal to examine or consider any evidence that is available. This blindness holds true not only in the realm of faith, but also in the area of skepticism.

Do you believe that the Bible is God's Word, or that it merely *contains* God's Word? Your answer is supremely important, for if you hold to the latter view, I believe that you will always vacillate between blind skepticism and blind trust in regards to any given verse or principle taught in the Bible. I say blind, because as you seek to sort it all out you will have nothing to guide you but your own subjective judgment or the opinions, often uninformed, of others.

If we want a vibrant, flourishing faith, one that carries us through dark and difficult places, we must first come to a place of assurance and rest, a safe place where God and His Word stand true.

Prayer Time

Dear Heavenly Father,

Thank You for giving us Your eternal, perfect Word of Truth! Precious Spirit of Truth, I ask You to teach and guide me into all truth so that I may understand and receive those things You wish to reveal to me. Help me to be receptive to Your promptings, even when my flesh wants to resist. Strengthen my faith and convict me of any skepticism residing in my heart. All these things I pray in Jesus' name. Amen.

Cultivating Your Garden of Faith

Get It Straight:

1. What does biblical inspiration mean? What is the definition of inerrancy as related to the Scriptures?

2. List three historical tests that are applied to ancient literature. How have these tests added credibility to the Bible?

3. Read Isaiah 44:28–45:7, 13. When this prophecy was written, Cyrus would not be born for one hundred and fifty years! Look up biblical passages referring to Cyrus. (Use a concordance or Bible software.) Who was Cyrus? How did he fulfill the prophecy?

4. Read the following passages: Isaiah 35:5-6; Zechariah 9:9. Where is their New Testament fulfillment?

Head to Heart:

1. What do you believe about the Bible? Is it the inspired, inerrant Word of God; is it purely man's opinion about God; is it a mixture of both?

2. Regarding the above question: Why do you believe this? How did you reach this conclusion?

3. What difficult Bible passages have you personally struggled with? Have you sought answers to these problems? If so, where did you search? Did you resolve these problems? If not, where might you look for additional help?

4. What promises from the Bible do you cling to with assurance? Why do you believe them? On what evidence or on whose authority do you claim them?

You and God:

1. Do you wish you had greater faith in the Bible? Why or why not?

2. If you struggle with your beliefs regarding the Bible, are you willing to seek additional apologetic literature? Why or why not?

Scripture Memory

All Scripture is God-breathed and is useful for teaching, rebuking, correcting and training in righteousness, so that the man of God may be thoroughly equipped for every good work. (2 Timothy 3:16-17)

Personal Thoughts:

_____

_____

_____

_____

_____

Chapter 4

What Your Faith Means to God

All the nations you have made will come and worship
before you, O Lord; they will bring glory to your name.
(Psalm 86:9)

Prior to my adopting Giggles, she had spent her entire life in a cage. Having the run of my bedroom was a new experience for my rescue-bunny, so she was understandably shy and timid in her unfamiliar environment. Whenever I approached her, she hopped away. When I finally cornered her, I gently stroked her and soothingly reassured her she had nothing to fear from me. I would provide for her every need, take good care of her and keep her from all harm. She was still afraid of me, and it hurt. During her first days with me I spent thirty minutes at a time petting her so she would get used to me. Eventually she relaxed and started "purring." Later in the day, thinking I had finally gotten through to her, I lovingly approached her, but once again she hopped away. At times, she let me pet her, but they were always on her terms. I felt sad because she couldn't trust me no matter how loving I was to her. The bonding process required time and patience, but eventually Giggles came around, and she now trusts me (except when I try to pick her up!)

My experience with Giggles helped me understand how God must feel when we shun Him. He lovingly cares for us, attentively watches over us, and provides for all our needs, yet we will not trust Him. God bestows blessing after blessing upon us, yet we do not see Him as our benefactor. As with Giggles, we would rather do our own thing or hide when we think He may want something from us. He derives great pleasure when we finally decide to trust Him, and what great joy, peace, and contentment we experience in return!

Faith Matters to God

God is not wishy-washy when it comes to our faith. The Scriptures affirm that faith is unequivocally important to Him. As we learned in a previous chapter, there are two aspects to faith:

- believing *in* God (He alone is the self-existent eternal God,— sovereign, omnipotent, compassionate; Jesus Christ is our Lord and Savior)

- believing God (His Word can be trusted; His motives are pure; our welfare is close to His heart)

Conversely, our lack of faith is equally displeasing to Him.

I am going to point out a number of Scriptures and tie them together in a manner that will enhance your awareness and appreciation of three essential truths:

- Our faith matters greatly to God.

- Unbelief carries weighty consequences

- You were created and called for a glorious purpose; your life has significance.

To Know and Believe

One of my favorite passages that reveals God's intense desire for His people to know and believe Him is found in the Old Testament book of Isaiah. Consider these verses carefully:

"You are my witnesses," declares the LORD,
"and my servant whom I have chosen,
so that you may know and believe me
and understand that I am he.
Before me no god was formed,
nor will there be one after me.
I, even I, am the LORD,
and apart from me there is no savior.
I have revealed and saved and proclaimed—
I, and not some foreign god among you.
You are my witnesses," declares the LORD, "that I am God.
Yes, and from ancient days I am he.
No one can deliver out of my hand.
When I act, who can reverse it?" (Isaiah 43:10-13)

LORD or *Yahovah* as it is rendered in Hebrew is the proper name of the one true God, Jehovah, meaning "the existing One." This is the name that God revealed to Moses on Mount Sinai when He made Himself known as: "I AM WHO I AM." This most sacred name of God identifies Him as the self-existing, covenant-keeping, eternal God, the same yesterday, today, and forever.

The Hebrew word for *God* or *god* is *el.* This is a more generic term for deity. It could refer to a person who is mighty in rank, power, strength, or nature, or it could be used in reference to a god either real (as in Jehovah, the one true God), or false (demons, imaginations, or anything worshiped as a god).

Do you see the significance of how the words *Lord, God,* and *god* are used? Jehovah is indisputably declaring that He is the one true God; there has never been any other real or imagined god in existence, nor will there ever be. There is no one else who can make a proclamation or revelation that is trustworthy and true; no one other than God has the power to save. He alone is sovereign, and no one can deter Him from what He has determined to do.

Another significant word used here is the verb to *know.* One of the most astounding revelations is that our Lord and God genuinely desires for us to know Him. The Hebrew word for know is *yada.* This term refers to a very close, personal level of familiarity one might have with another individual, and it was often used to represent the intimate relationship between a husband and wife.

I would also like you to recognize that God *chose* (or called) *them* (us) to be His *servants* and *witnesses.*

These verses overflow with extraordinary declarations, don't they? Notice how often they are repeated. Redundancy is utilized here for the sake of emphasis, and God does not want us to miss it. These passages are affirming in no uncertain terms that God chose the Israelites (and ultimately you and me as Abraham's spiritual offspring— see Romans 9:8 and Galatians 3:28-29) as both His witnesses and servants, so that they (we) would develop a reverent yet intimate knowledge of Him, learn to trust Him implicitly, and believe that He alone is the sovereign eternal God and Savior of all peoples.

Seeking God

The New Testament author of Hebrews forthrightly tells the Jewish Christians that believing in God (that He exists) and believing God (trusting and seeking) are important to Him. Without either one, we cannot please Him.

*And without faith it is impossible to please God, because anyone
who comes to him must believe that he exists and that he rewards
those who earnestly seek him. (Hebrews 11:6)*

The faith referred to through the words *must believe* relates to
what we would call "saving-faith."

Our word *must* comes from the Greek word *dei*. In this context
it signifies the following: "of necessity arising from the determinate
will and counsel of God, ...especially regarding the salvation of
men through the Death, Resurrection and Ascension of Christ."[1]

Ekzeteo, the New Testament Greek word for *seek*, means to search
for diligently. It also may be translated: to investigate, to scrutinize,
to require. I especially love the next two definitions: to beg, to crave.

What a rich word this is! If I am searching for God in the manner
that this passage depicts, I am seeking Him diligently with all of
my heart because my very being craves Him. I realize that having
Him in my life is more than just a desire; it is a hunger and a thirst
driven by the realization that my existence is meaningless, empty,
and dry without Him. It means that I want to learn as much about
Him as I can because I intensely desire to have an intimate yet
reverent knowledge of Him.

This kind of attitude delights God. Apathy and half-heartedness
is not pleasing to Him. Notice the strong warning Christ gave to the
Church in Laodicea. "So, because you are **lukewarm**—neither hot
nor cold—I am about to **spit** you out of my mouth" (Revelation 3:16).

The Greek words that we translate lukewarm and spit are very
striking indeed: *Chliaros* means *tepid, lukewarm,* but it was also used
as a metaphor to describe the condition of the soul wretchedly
fluctuating between a torpor (inertia) and a fervor of love. E*meo*, used
here for *spit*, is more accurately translated to vomit, to throw up.

The very idea that my apathetic, indecisive oscillating devotion toward Christ is nauseating to Him is indeed a sobering and heartbreaking thought.

Please don't brush over the wonderful truths expressed in these Old and New Testament verses. God is revealing His heart. The infinite Creator of this vast and complex universe is a relational God, and He wants to have a deep, intimate relationship with you and me. God, by His very nature, knows absolutely everything about each one of us, but He earnestly desires that you and I develop a reverential intimacy with Him too. And as we get to know Him better, our faith and trust in Him will grow.

Does this sound incredible to you? Has God seemed remote and unapproachable to you? If that has been your experience, I understand—I was there. I used to regard Christ as little more than fire insurance. But regardless of what you may think now, our Lord is a God that you can know, and as you continue on this faith journey, I urge you to ask Him to help you in this process. He delights in our pursuit of Him and faithfully promises to reward us as we seek Him in this manner; He vows that we will be satisfied. According to the Old Testament promise, He makes Himself known to those who sincerely seek Him (Jeremiah 29:12-14).

The Consequences of Unbelief

To further develop the importance of faith from God's perspective, I would like us to look at a few more passages of Scripture.

A Garden Full of Heartaches

Back in the Garden of Eden, Satan's first utterance was "Did God really say? …" (Genesis 3:1). Eve's problem was not that she doubted God's existence. Up to that time she and Adam had enjoyed a wonderfully intimate relationship with their Creator. Eve's faithlessness demonstrated itself in her failure to believe what God had told them. Satan convinced Eve to doubt the purity of God's motives, thereby casting doubt on His very character. A weakening of faith in turn led Adam and Eve to believe that perhaps God was holding out on them—that His commands were not really for their welfare.

The entire human race is still suffering the repercussions of Adam and Eve's faithless disobedience.

Death in the Desert

The author of Hebrews implores New Testament believers to apply to themselves the account of what happened to the Israelites in the desert. These verses include a chilling warning for those who continue on in their unbelief: (Hebrews 3:12, 15-19).

God wanted to bless the Israelites by bringing them victoriously into the Promised Land, but they rebelled and refused to believe, and they were never allowed to enter. There were no atheists in the desert. They had witnessed the ten plagues God had unleashed upon the Egyptians; they had experienced the parting of the Red Sea; they had seen water come out of a rock; they had observed the pillar of fire by night and the cloud by day, and these are only a few of the many miracles they observed on their journey to the Promised Land. Yet every time life in the desert became difficult, they whimpered and whined.

When the day came for them to enter into the Promised Land they refused to do so out of fear, having believed the negative reports brought back by ten of the twelve spies. God finally reached His breaking point with the Israelites. He prohibited those who were twenty years or older (excluding Joshua and Caleb, the two faithful spies) from ever entering the Promised Land. Forty years later, after that unbelieving generation had died, God, through Joshua, safely led their children into the Promised Land. You can read this painful narrative in chapters thirteen and fourteen of the book of Numbers.

They murmured and complained constantly. They either had too much of something or not enough; they pined for the "good ol' days" of slavery and threatened rebellion time and time again. Yet the author of Hebrews, writing to the first century Hebrew Christians, sums up the sins of the Israelites in one word: **unbelief!**

The Greek word for unbelief is *apistia* (noun) or *apistos* (adjective) and refers to weakness of faith as well as unfaithfulness. It describes one who is lacking in faith or refers to a thing that is not to be believed. Note in particular these next two meanings: without trust in God, not worthy of confidence.

God...not worthy of our confidence?

He who did not spare his own Son, but gave him up for us all—how will he not also, along with him, graciously give us all things? (Romans 8:32)

At the cross God proved Himself worthy of our confidence! We may not say it aloud, but every time we flippantly make decisions without considering God's will, stubbornly hang on to our rights, assert our independence from Him, blame God for failing to come through for us, complain about our lives, try to fix our problems by our own methods, turn to prayer only as a last resort, we are shouting in the ears of God, "You are not worthy of my confidence!"

Waves of Doubt

James, the half-brother of Jesus, implores his readers whenever they struggle under great trials, to seek God and ask for wisdom in handling their situation. James assures them that God will gladly give them His wisdom. But he sternly warns them that God will give nothing to those who waver back and forth in their doubt. (Read James 1:5-8).

This New Testament letter was written to saved and sanctified Jewish Christians, those who had already put their faith in Jesus

Christ. Their salvation was not being questioned in these verses. James is referring to the blessings and victories available to them—and to us—in this life.

The verses reveal the fact that we can believe in Christ, acknowledge that He died for our sins, receive eternal salvation, and at the same time live as practical atheists by failing to stand firm in our faith, going along with the world's philosophies, not enduring our trials with hope, and refusing to prove Him trustworthy in our daily lives.

Is our faith important to God? Can our unbelief and doubt cancel out the rich blessings that God planned for us to enjoy during our earthly life? According to the God's Word, absolutely!

I'm glad you are staying with me through some in-depth Bible study, including the Greek and Hebrew lexicons. One of my goals is to help you to transfer the theological knowledge you acquire from your head to your heart as you come to realize that God wants a living, vital relationship with you. As you read this chapter, please understand that your faith is radically important to God. If you have an image of God as a gentle, permissive grandfather who winks at your unbelief, you will never be motivated to deepen your faith.

Your Calling and Purpose in Life

The fact that God deeply values our faith is further exemplified as we investigate the reasons that He created us in the first place. The following Scripture references shed much light on this. Consider the first of these.

> *You are worthy, our Lord and God,*
> *to receive glory and honor and power,*
> *for you created all things,*
> *and by your will they were created*
> *and have their being. (Revelation 4:11)*

The Greek word for *glory* here is *doxa*. It means opinion, judgment, or estimate. In the New Testament it always refers to a good opinion of someone, resulting in praise and honor. In addition it signifies splendor, brightness, and majesty. This would be His kingly majesty—the absolute perfection of deity—that belongs to Him as the supreme creator and ruler of all.

God's infinite glory surpasses anything you or I can comprehend and is beyond anything we can define, describe, or imagine. His glory not only reflects Him; it is His very essence! It is the way He makes himself known or shows Himself mighty.

The Greek word for *will* is *thelema*. It signifies choice, inclination, desire, **pleasure.** This verse tells us that we were created for God's pleasure. He created us to give Him praise and honor because He is the maker and sustainer of all things. Have you ever thought about your existence in those terms?

This same thought is expressed by Paul in his letter to the Corinthians: "So whether you eat or drink or whatever you do, do it all for the *glory* of God" (1 Corinthians 10:31).

Here is an Old Testament verse to consider:

*For you are a people holy to the LORD your God. The LORD your God has chosen you out of all the peoples on the face of the earth to be **his people**, **his treasured possession.** (Deuteronomy 7:6)*

You are God's workmanship, His prize masterpiece! He desires to display the glory of His being, His spectacular attributes, His magnificent works to you, but He also wishes to reveal them through you—and therein comes the calling.

You were created and commissioned by the Father for the purpose of bringing glory, fame, and honor to the very name and nature of God. By your existence His reputation, His honor, and His glory are displayed not only throughout the entire earth, but to the angels in the Heavenly realms. He has staked His reputation on us to do just that, and God invites you to share with Him to that end. What an incredible invitation!

There are numerous New Testament parallels to this concept. I have listed four for you to read.

- Ephesians 1:4
- Ephesians 1:11-12
- Ephesians 2:10
- 2 Peter 1:3

From these verses we can see that God created us by His will to do His will for the purpose of His pleasure and glory.

As the Scripture verses presented to you in this chapter reveal, God's reputation, His renown, His glory, and His honor are very important to Him, and yet, as perplexing as this is to us, He often lets them ride on flawed and fickle people who He knows cannot live up to the calling. Sadly, when the Jews failed to be worthy witnesses (and that also applies to us), the other nations mocked the God of Israel (Romans 2: 23-24).

What an amazing, merciful, and forgiving God we have through our Lord and Savior, Jesus Christ! Throughout the ages we have trampled God's glory and dragged His very name through the mud. Yet God, because of Jesus' atoning sacrifice for our sins, has not rejected us. Those who fall upon His grace, He pulls out of the mire, cleans up, dresses in fine linen, and restores to their position as His royal children. Who can comprehend it!

This is love: not that we loved God, but that he loved
us and sent his Son as an atoning sacrifice for our sins.
(1 John 4:10)

Connecting the Dots:

Let's tie these concepts together before moving on to the role that faith plays.

- God created us (the ultimate reason and purpose for our existence)
    - ~ for His pleasure (to please Him).
    - ~ to give Him glory and honor (to praise and worship Him for who His is and for His mighty works).
    - ~ to bring Him glory and honor (as His masterpiece).
    - ~ to do good works.

- Similarly, God chose us (called us)
    - ~ to be His witnesses (to uphold His honor and name before the nations).
    - ~ to be His servants (to do His will).
    - ~ to know Him (intimately and to have a meaningful relationship with Him).
    - ~ to be His people and His treasured possession (to lavish His love, tender care, mercies, and grace upon us).
    - ~ to believe Him (to trust Him).
    - ~ to believe in Him (that He alone is the eternal sovereign God).
    - ~ to be holy and blameless (to be godly in character).
    - ~ for the praise of His glory (proclaiming and displaying His glory).
- Without faith it is impossible to please Him.
- God desires us to earnestly seek Him.
- God rewards those who seek Him with all their heart.

The Role of Faith

Faith is the key to all of this. We cannot please God or honor Him if we refuse to believe in Him or if we choose not to trust Him. If we fail to exercise our faith, the whole purpose of our lives is negated, and the reason that He has called us becomes futile. Is it any wonder that when our faith in God is at its lowest, we feel empty, dead, and hopeless inside? For it is during those times that our lives lose their very meaning and purpose.

Faith is essential for another extremely important reason. It is the *only way in which we are able to be obedient and thus glorify God.*

The kind of life-changing faith I am talking about goes beyond believing in certain facts; it must be living and tangible. James acknowledged this when he wrote:What good is it, my brothers, if a man claims to have faith but has no deeds? Can such faith save him? …Faith by itself, if it is not accompanied by action, is dead. (James 2:14, 17)

Scripture clearly affirms that *we can never earn our salvation through righteous acts* (see Ephesians 2:8-9). James' point is that true faith *results* in a changed life and good deeds. Faith transforms our conduct as well as our thoughts. True faith must result in action—growing in Christian character, practicing moral discipline, developing perseverance, doing God's will, loving others—or it will surely wither and die.

If faith is the only way we can bring glory to God, how do we get there? The apostle Paul acknowledged the sad truth about mankind when he wrote, "For all have sinned and fall short of the glory of God" (Romans 3:23).

Paul informs us in Colossians 1:26-27 that there is no hope for God's glory to be displayed by any of us apart from Christ, no matter how valiant of an effort we make, for it is "Christ in [us]" (the Holy Spirit dwelling within us) who *enables* us to demonstrate God's spectacular glory.

In another letter Paul tells us a life that glorifies God is a process that develops slowly with time. As we grow in faith and learn to trust in and cooperate with the Holy Spirit, we will be more *willing* to allow Him to work God's glory in our lives. We will see a continual increase of moral purity and holiness in our lives as God's character becomes increasingly visible in us (2 Corinthians 3:18).

How is our road trip together going for you? Are you feeling the bumps? If so, please do not become overwhelmed or discouraged by such lofty expectations of righteousness. As I mentioned before, none of us can possibly live up to them.

Deciding to trust in God is very difficult. But don't despair! God understands our unbelief, and He is very eager to help us overcome any skepticism, doubt, and cynicism. God hears and answers our prayers when we come to Him in honesty and simply admit that we lack confidence in Him. Like the father of the demon-possessed boy (Mark 9:14-29), He longs to hear us cry out, "I do believe; help me overcome my unbelief!"

God in His mercy empowers us to grow in our faith so that we can become all that He created us to be, and it begins by taking our focus off ourselves and putting it onto Christ (Hebrews 12:1-2).

Jesus is the originator of our faith. He is the source of life, salvation, and faith—the very faith needed by us to endure hardships and temptations. Jesus is also the perfecter of our faith; He is the one who not only grows our faith so that we can become disentangled from sinful patterns in our lives and pursue a godly life, but He is the one who will bring it fully to completion.

Your part is to ask Him to increase your faith and to cooperate with the Holy Spirit in this exciting and worthy endeavor. Do not get discouraged; God will assist you in your search. He is most willing to help you triumph over your skepticism.

Being confident of this, that he who began a good work in you will carry it on to completion until the day of Christ Jesus. (Philippians 1:6)

Prayer Time

O sovereign God, Creator of all that exists,
You are marvelous beyond comparison. I confess that my heart grows cold at times. Please help me to hear and respond to Your voice so that I never become hardened by sin's deceitfulness—or waver in my faith. Help me to bring glory and honor to Your name by my actions and words. Amen.

Cultivating Your Garden of Faith

Get It Straight:

1. What does it mean to seek God, and why does that please Him?

2. We have discussed two reasons why faith is an essential ingredient to fulfilling our purpose and meaning in life. What are they?

Read Psalm 8; Psalm 102:12, 15; and Psalm 86:8-10, then answer the following questions:

3. What are some of the ways that God's glory and majesty are manifested?

4. How is the concept of God's glory, honor, and majesty expressed?

5. How has God bestowed glory and honor on humankind?

Head to Heart:

1. What emotions did you experience as you read the bulleted list on page 64 depicting the reasons God created and chose us?

2. Read again Colossians 1:26-27; 2 Corinthians 3:18; and Hebrews 12:1-2. According to these passages, what role does the Triune God play as we seek to honor and glorify Him? What is our responsibility? How does this encourage you?

You and God:

1. God longs for an intimate relationship with you? Does this scare you? Why or why not?

2. What things about your life bring glory and honor to God (thoughts, attitudes, words, behaviors)? How does this make you feel?

3. What things in your life are not God-honoring?

4. Humility means proper respect for God, not self-deprecation. How can the verses in Psalm 8 help set you free from feelings of worthlessness?

Scripture Memory

And without faith it is impossible to please God, because anyone who comes to him must believe that he exists and that he rewards those who earnestly seek him. (Hebrews 11:6)

Personal Thoughts:

Chapter 5

Feeling Let Down by God

O my God, I cry by day, but You do not answer;
And by night, but I have no rest. (Psalm 22:2, NASB)

When my husband, David, was nine years old, his teacher organized a Christmas gift exchange for the class. She asked each student to bring an anonymous gift costing no more than five dollars. David was excited about the upcoming exchange and the following weekend shopped with his mother at the toy store. They picked out the perfect gift. The day before Christmas break, the teacher began handing out the presents; excited chatter filled the room! David's smile faded quickly as he stared with horror at his gift. Wrapped in brightly colored paper was a pair of silk socks! Disappointed beyond belief, David cried all the way home.

Life throws many disappointments and sorrows at us along with varying degrees of anguish. But whether they result in mere frustration or leave us grieving in utter despair, they all stand ready to shake our faith and tell us that God has let us down.

Many Christians live with persistent heartaches. They may reside close to the surface of their soul or lay hidden deep in their heart.

They may be known by everyone or by no one; nevertheless, they are there—raw and painful. Their lives are not necessarily falling apart. They may have friends, family, a good job, adequate finances, good health; still, there is something unattainable that they yearn for. They cannot buy it or earn it. No matter how much they plan, persevere, struggle, manipulate, or cry, it remains out of reach. Perhaps one of the most painful things about their elusive dream is the fact that it is a noble and good desire that would seemingly add quality to their lives and the lives of others around them.

Can you identify? Perhaps you are single and want a spouse to share your life with. Maybe you and your spouse can't have children, and even adoption plans have failed time and again. Possibly you have loved ones who scoff at God, and no matter how earnestly you pray they remain cynical and cold toward Him. Could it be that there is an education you long to pursue or a career field you have not been able to get into? You may have a son with a drug addiction or a daughter who openly scorns you. It may be that you have an incapacitated parent, child, or spouse that you must constantly care for. After years of struggling to solve your problem, you have finally come to the conclusion that you are powerless over this. God alone can answer your heartfelt prayer, but up to this point He has not done so. What are we to do in such situations … give up on our dreams … give up on God? Can we hold on to both without the strain breaking our hearts in two?"

If you have experienced disappointment and frustration with God, how did you respond? Did you talk to God about your feelings, or did you pretend they did not exist? Maybe you were ashamed of your "blasphemous" thoughts, so you stuffed them into a hole somewhere deep in your soul. In spite of your suffering did you continue to praise God? Perhaps your pain was so intense and your disappointment so real you turned your face from Him and simply walked away. If you gave up on God, I can relate because I did.

A Personal Story of Disappointment

I experienced disappointment with God for the first thirty-eight years of my life. As a young child, I lacked confidence and seemed to fail at everything I tried. I was shy, ill at ease, and had a hard time concentrating in the classroom. I was terrified of speaking up or asking questions. I had been laughed at in the past and did not want to be vulnerable again. I received very poor grades through the sixth grade, and my classmates labeled me dumb.

I could not shrug off the ridicule. I craved acceptance, fearing rejection above all, and my feelings were often hurt. In order to cope I grew overly dependent upon my parents for security. I withdrew from others, and the price I paid was great loneliness and continued feelings of inadequacy.

In despair I sometimes turned to God, but my concept of Him was small, selfish, and terribly distorted. I saw Him as a spiritual Santa Claus. I believed that Jesus died for my sins, yet I never grasped the significance of the cross. I did not realize that Jesus wanted to be the Lord and Master of my life or that He desired to have a personal relationship with me. Instead I believed that God was deeply disappointed in me, and during times of despair I felt totally rejected by Him.

I'd read parts of the Bible, but it was confusing to me, so I decided that if God wanted me to know something, He would have to make it clear to my mind.

I grew more distant from God and decided if I were going to succeed, I would have to do it on my own. In my late teens, I read self-help books and began replacing fear and doubt with self-determination. I loved the success I experienced, and I quickly became a compulsive overachiever. I discovered I had an introspective, analytical mind suited perfectly for computer logic. I became a successful software engineer, yet I couldn't shake the fear that my success was phony and someday I would be "found out." What a terrible price I paid to ensure that this would never happen: an all-consuming drive for accomplishment and perfectionism, an obsession with my appearance, an out-of-control eating disorder, a self-centered focus, a prideful spirit, and incessant guilt.

In my mid- to late- thirties, I hit a deep, dark place in my life. Mounting stress and emotional insecurity finally got to me. I began experiencing marital problems, and feelings of worthlessness overwhelmed me. Life seemed empty and meaningless. My professional accomplishments offered little satisfaction, and I felt like a complete failure.

I prayed to my Santa Claus God for help but received none. In my anger, I turned completely away from God and everything I had cherished. My rebellious actions led to a moral collapse. The guilt, shame, and self-condemnation consumed me, and I was certain that if anyone knew who I really was, I would be rejected, so I isolated myself from others, just as I had so many years before.

Where Are You God?

Your life experiences may be completely different, but at some point you may have shared my question. "Where were You, God, when I needed You?"

According to the Bible, God is steadfast and faithful.

He will cover you with his feathers, and under his wings you will find refuge; his faithfulness will be your shield and rampart. (Psalm 91:4)

How do we account for those times when God seemed to abandon us? Has the Bible misled us? Have we uncovered *unfaithfulness* in God?

Let me suggest one or more things that may have been at work. I will discuss each in greater depth later in this book. For now I will briefly list them for you to mull over:

- You misconstrued God's promises and failed to understand the conditions and warnings attached to those promises.

- You misinterpreted His answer to you. Perhaps you didn't understand how the apparent disaster was designed to bring blessing in your life; because the "why" didn't make sense, maybe you failed to ask and receive an answer to the more important question, "To what end?"

- And ... my personal favorite: You rushed ahead of God and took matters into your hands, failing to wait upon His perfect timing.

I've come to the conclusion that God loves "suspense." Here we are, minding our own business, when suddenly Satan comes along, binds us up, and throws us on the railroad tracks of life. Then, just seconds before the train runs over us, God swoops down and pulls us off the tracks.

God often waits until the very last minute in order to teach us a lesson in trust. But through it all, He wants us to do our part, not His part. If we insist on rushing ahead of God in order to "fix" the situation, we will never experience His faithfulness. Instead we will be left with a mess on our hands wondering why God didn't rescue us.

But sometimes the train does run over us—at least it sure seems to!

When God Answers No

John and Kay Anderson are anxiously sitting in the waiting room of a large metropolitan hospital after being notified that their son, Mark, was involved in a serious industrial accident. John is an elder in the church. Kay leads a women's Bible study. The church prayer chain is in action. The pastor is at the hospital along with several other elders. Huddled together Pastor Steve leads the group in fervent prayer for Mark's life. About ninety minutes later the surgeon approaches. He places a hand on John's quivering shoulder and says, "We just finished operating on your son. Mark is going to be all right." The group utters a joyful cry. Both John and Pastor Steve blurt out, "Praise God!" Kay drops instantly to her knees. Hugging the chair and weeping with relief she cries out, "Thank You, God. Praise You, Jesus. You are so good. Thank you for your mercy and goodness. Thank you for sparing Mark." The group continues to rejoice and praise God.

About three days later, another godly family huddles together in a different wing of that same hospital. They are joined by their pastor and several close friends. They are praying ardently together for the life of Dale Martin's wife, Kim, and their newborn son. What should have been a joyous occasion is quickly turning into a nightmare as mother and baby fight for their lives. Dale is a youth pastor, and the entire youth group is gathered at the church in prayer for Dale, Kim, and their son. Later that evening, the doctor grimly approaches Dale, his parents, and Kim's parents. "I'm deeply sorry. We were unable to save your wife and son." Kim's mother collapses in her husband's arms and begins to weep uncontrollably. Dale's father and mother hug their son in an attempt to comfort him while the pastor lovingly spreads his arms around the grieving families.

Two families who love God and honor Him with their lives: only one of the families leaves the hospital rejoicing. But what about the precious family whose heartfelt prayers were answered with a "no"? How do they deal with their grief and loss? How are they to view God's love, grace, and mercy?

In our limited window of understanding it is impossible to explain why an all-knowing, all-powerful, good, and loving God would allow a godly family to be torn apart by two untimely deaths. We must go to God's Word to understand how He wants us to interpret the painful, unavoidable circumstances that occur all too often in this fallen world.

When life deals us crushing blows we are forced to ask ourselves: "Do I really believe the Scriptures are the authoritative, inspired Word of God? Can I trust them to be true in spite of my circumstances, regardless of what my emotions are telling me, despite what others around me are saying?" Inevitably we are left with the following decision: Will I retain a divine vantage even though I don't understand, or will I attempt to interpret circumstances through my perspective?

The most devastating loss a Christian can experience is the death of one's faith. Can you believe that God is doing something consequential and purposeful through your sorrow? God is asking, "Do you trust Me?" Your entire Christian walk boils down to the issue of answering this all-important question.

Conditional Trust

What do you fear most? Is it losing your job? Perhaps it is an unfaithful spouse or a devastating illness. How about failure, bankruptcy, or growing old and feeble? Could it be getting a divorce or losing your home? Maybe your fear centers on the untimely death of a loved one.

Do you have a mental list of potential disasters you are certain you could not survive? How does God fit into your thinking? Are you trusting Him to never allow these things to happen to you? If so, you may be setting yourself up for inconsolable despair.

I am grateful for the teaching of author and Bible teacher Beth Moore on the subject of conditional trust. She pinpointed a core issue: Many of us say we trust God, but in reality our trust in Him is shallow and conditional at best.

It is not enough to trust God that the thing we most fear will never happen. In fact, that is *not* trust at all! When we do this we are essentially telling God, "I will trust You to do as I direct." We may not consciously say this, but deep down in our thinking God has become our servant instead of our Master.

If that is the basis of our faith, we can count on at least two things:

First, Satan will bring this fear to the surface of our minds, because he knows the threat of it becoming a reality is all we need to become incapacitated. In reality, most things we spend our lives dreading will probably never happen. Anytime Satan wants us out of the way, all he has to do is manufacture a little faulty "evidence" to make us believe that the thing we fear is imminent. Test yourself on this. Make a list of all the things you told God you could never survive were they to happen. You will probably find that the enemy threatens you with these things time and again.

Second, conditional trust leaves us devastatingly vulnerable. Over the years we come to believe that the perceived crisis would utterly destroy us. In our fearful minds we place demands upon God and comfort ourselves with the false hope that He will obey our will. We convince ourselves that a loving God would never allow this dreadful thing to occur. We say things such as, "I love God and try to obey Him; surely He will prevent this tragedy from happening."

Here is the risk: What if, in God's eternal perspective and His infinite wisdom, He makes a different proclamation over our lives—one we will never understand in this lifetime. We will be devastated and our faith in God destroyed, all because we told God it was the one thing we could never survive.

The Bible implores us to view these potential fears in another way:

Surely he will never be shaken; a righteous man will be remembered forever. He will have no fear of bad news; his heart is steadfast, trusting in the Lord. His heart is secure, he will have no fear; in the end he will look in triumph on his foes. (Psalm 112:6-8)

The Hebrew word for steadfast in Psalm 112 is *kuwn*. It means to be established, stable, and secure, to be enduring, prepared, settled.

Notice what the text says about bad news. The righteous man will not fear it. Not because he will never receive any, but because he is prepared and ready to endure the bad news should it come. He is able to bear it because he is stable and secure in his trust in the Lord. The truth is sometimes we do get bad news. Deep hurts happen. But unconditional trust says, "I choose to trust you, God, no matter what."

The righteous woman endures bad news because she believes two things: First, even if her worst nightmare happens, she knows God must have a purpose behind it. There must have been some gigantic glory at stake or a sorely needed ministry. Through tears she affirms, "You created me with a purpose; my life is meant to have meaning. With Your help I'll get back up. If it's Your plan for me I will minister to people who are going through similar pain. I will give hope to those who wonder how they are going to survive." Second, if what she fears happens, she knows that God will strengthen her. The "bad news" will not tear her apart. She is trusting God to take care of her so that she will not only survive but be victorious.

Years ago one of my eyes suddenly became bloodshot, and the stabbing pain drove me to see an ophthalmologist without delay. The doctor diagnosed it as acute iritis, a disease that can cause blindness if left untreated. The doctor listed several possible causes, but when he said the words *autoimmune disease,* my panicked mind shut out everything else he said.

My mother died after struggling with rheumatoid arthritis for twenty years. I had watched her go from healthy and vibrant to diseased and feeble within a matter of months. The fear of inheriting her illness remained with me, and now the dreaded "proof" that I inherited this disease was close at hand. Ten months later a second outbreak in my eyes took my level of fear to new proportions.

I will never forget the drive home from the ophthalmologist. Fearful images cycled through my mind, but thankfully they were no match for God. As His thoughts broke though my own, I knew He was asking me to trust Him. I had been living with dread for more than twenty years, and it was time to put it to death. Alone in my kitchen, I knelt down on the hardwood floor and tearfully handed my fear over to God, giving Him "permission" to be Lord over this matter. If I never developed this disease I would praise Him; if I did, I would trust Him to help me bear it with confidence and peace, knowing that, through this illness, He would bring opportunities for me to glorify Him. Either way, I would be fine, because He would always be with me.

That morning I arose with a new sense of peace and freedom. Since that day I have not feared illness of any kind. I never had another attack in my eyes, and thus far in my life I am free from autoimmune disease. Satan could no longer paralyze me with fear.

God eagerly desires to do the same for you, but He needs your unconditional trust. Will you turn your deepest fears over to God and let Him cultivate a flourishing faith within the soil of your heart?

An End to My Searching

After the moral collapse I referred to earlier, I desperately wanted peace with God, but I didn't know how to obtain it. I reasoned that if I could only become a better person, then God would accept me and help me out of the mess I had made of my life. But no matter how earnestly I tried, I couldn't fix myself. I couldn't make myself worthy enough to approach God. I tried to pray, but all I got was complete silence. Had I gone too far to ever be loved by God again? For the first time in my life I was terrified of dying—absolutely petrified that I would spend eternity in hell. The fear and shame went on for nearly a year until one rainy December morning.

I had pulled out onto my driveway to go to work when it started to drizzle. I sat there in my car for a full five minutes before deciding which umbrella to take: the conventional type or the tiny fold-up kind. Finally, I headed to work. About halfway there, I realized I had left my lunch at home. I drove around the block several times trying to decide whether to go home and get my lunch or buy something in the cafeteria. I finally realized I could save my company a lot of money by calling in sick that day.

Losing the ability to make trivial decisions really scared me, so I made an appointment with a Christian counselor. I poured out all of my grief and shame to him. When I finished, he assured me that, through Christ, God would accept me just as I was. He encouraged me to stop struggling with trying to be good. Instead, he urged me to submit myself to God and let God be the one to change me. He told me to go home and write down all my sins. After that I was to talk with God about everything on the list, acknowledging that these things were wrong and ask for His forgiveness. I was to thank Jesus for dying for me on the cross, surrender my will to Him, and ask Him to take control of my life. But it was what he told me to do afterward with the list that surprised me the most. Being an analytical person, I had expected him to have me review the paper once a week, analyzing the progress I had or had not made. Imagine my surprise when he told me to burn it!

December 8, 1987, I wrote out my list and prayed, desperately hanging on to what the counselor had said about God accepting me as I was, clinging to the promise that it would be God who would change me. I knelt in front of my fireplace, watching the paper go up in flames. My heart was broken and humbled. I prayed earnestly. For the first time I felt God's loving presence enfold me. I couldn't stop praying; my communion with God was more precious than anything I had ever experienced. I wanted to make those moments last forever. At some point I realized that all my guilt was gone. I felt clean, forgiven, and totally accepted by God. I was astonished! All my life I'd had problems dealing with guilt. But now, for the first time ever, I was guilt-free. That's when I knew for certain that the supernatural power of God had done its work. My heart found the confirmation it was seeking. I was indeed loved by God. Gratitude flooded my soul!

For a few weeks, God was all I could think about. I wanted to get home from work in order to spend time alone with Him. I wanted to learn everything I could about this merciful God. As I opened my Bible and began reading, I was astounded. There it was, the very thing I had been seeking all my life! God's assurance that He would never reject or abandon me; His faithful promise to meet my deepest needs and sustain me in my dark hours. Through His Word, the glory and beauty of who He is shone with more clarity and brilliance than a sea full of diamonds: His infinite knowledge and wisdom, His awesome power and supreme sovereignty over His creation, His incomprehensible holiness, His purity, righteousness, and justice—all this coupled with unfailing forgiveness, unfathomable mercy and grace, immeasurable compassion, tender-hearted kindness, and a steadfast love that defies human imagination.

About three weeks later I took a good look at myself and couldn't believe what I saw. I had become a brand new person. The old diseased thoughts and desires that had led to my moral collapse were totally gone. My thinking, attitudes, desires, even my interests had been completely changed. The person I had been only a few weeks earlier had become like a stranger to me.

In Christ I had finally found the unconditional love and acceptance I had been seeking all my life along with a precious relationship that has lead me to the greatest adventures of my life. In some ways my life has become more difficult. Yet even in times of trouble, I have a sense of hope and joy that I never had before because I know that God will sustain me. My life now has a meaning and purpose that has nothing to do with my accomplishments. It's all about God. I used to experience brief satisfaction from my endeavors, but I always had to outdo myself or else feelings of inadequacy would return. But now, just meditating on God's accomplishments and what He has done for me gives me a sense of excitement that does not grow stale.

As painful as my past sins are to me, I love remembering and reliving that wonderful night more than twenty years ago, for it always rekindles my love for our Savior. It is still difficult at times for me to comprehend His unconditional love for me, but I thank God that He does. "Thanks be to God for his indescribable gift!" (2 Corinthians 9:15).

Trusting God in all Life's Circumstances

God promises to give you His best too. In every situation you face, God wants you to realize He has not forgotten you. If a relentless longing is causing sorrow in your life, be comforted. Intense desire coupled with delayed answer to prayer can drive you into a deep and sweet fellowship with God. If your life is scarred by tragedy, take heart, for our Lord is the Father of compassion and the God of all comfort (2 Corinthians 1:3). If the fear of impending disaster has you paralyzed, take courage; for Christ has promised to bind up the broken hearted and free all captives from their chains of fear (Isaiah 61:1, Luke 4:18).

God asks us to interpret our circumstances by His love, rather than the other way around. If you let God work in your life, your painful experiences will result in untold blessings. It is imperative for us to come to a place of peace regarding our circumstances or our faith in God will always be crippled and we will live in fear, constantly anxious about our future.

Prayer Time

Father,

Grant me wisdom and understanding that I may be filled with hope. Strengthen my trust in You and create in me a faith that flourishes. I will trust You to get me through anything that happens in my life. Not only will I endure heartaches, but I will be triumphant over them. I pray these things in Jesus Christ, my Rock and my Fortress (Psalm 62:2). Amen.

Cultivating Your Garden of Faith

Get It Straight:

1. Look up the following passages. Compose a list of benefits or results of trusting God: Psalm 22:4; Psalm 28:7; Psalm 32:10; Psalm 33:21; Psalm 37:3-5; Psalm 52:8; Psalm 56:11; Psalm 112:7; Psalm 115:9-11; Psalm 125:1; Proverbs 29:25; Isaiah 12:2; Isaiah 25:9; Isaiah 26:3-4; Jeremiah 17:7; Nahum 1:7; John 14:1; Romans 10:11; Romans 15:13.

2. Read Psalm 22 (written by King David). This is the Psalm Jesus quoted from the cross. Notice how many verses specifically apply to Christ's suffering. In verses 1-10 David (and Christ) express great agony and despair; verses 11-21 contain David's prayer along with further declarations of anguish; verses 22-31 record his praises. There is a huge shift in David's mood after this prayer. What does David ask God for? What specific praises does he give to God?

Head to Heart:

1. Do you think calling out to God and praising Him while suffering (as David and Christ did) will strengthen you and lessen your distress? Why or why not?

2. When life deals you crushing blows, what are the first things you tend to think and do? At what point do you usually turn to God and His Word?

You and God:

1. Is there something good you desperately long for? Has this need driven you to pray or to resist prayer? Has the delay strengthened or weakened your faith? In what ways?

2. What are your deepest fears? Does the enemy taunt you with them? Pray right now. Reviewing the benefits of placing your trust in God. Ask Him to deliver you from these fears and give you peace.

Scripture Memory

Why are you downcast, O my soul? Why so disturbed within me? Put your hope in God, for I will yet praise him, my Savior and my God. (Psalm 42:11)

Personal Thoughts:

Chapter 6

What Are You Doing, God?

Consider it pure joy, my brothers, whenever you face
trials of many kinds, because you know that the testing
your faith develops perseverance. Perseverance must finish
its work so that you may be mature and complete, not
lacking anything. (James 1:2-4)

A dear friend from California, who is a single mom, sent me
the following e-mail:

I am doing ok, I guess. My foster daughter of 5 years went
off her meds and became a little psychotic. She checked
herself into a homeless shelter and is now living on the
streets and is pregnant. She thinks I am the cause of all her
problems, which is very hurtful.

Now, I have to short sale or foreclose on my home
because I no longer have the income and am not able to
get another foster child with my school schedule being
so hectic. I have one year left and I pray that I don't have
to quit for financial reasons. I am already in a lot of debt
because of educational expenses.

But, with God's help everything will work out. I just have to pray for the right attitude.

I love this house dearly and so love watching my kids jump on the trampoline and swim in the pool. The neighborhood kids enjoy playing here as well and I feel that I have a ministry by providing them with a safe place to play. But if it is not God's will, then I pray for patience and wisdom. Maybe, I am valuing this lifestyle more than God which is sometimes easy to do when you are in the lap of luxury. Maybe I need to come down a few pegs. Whatever the reason, please pray that I will keep a good attitude and continue to keep my eyes on the Lord. I do need to conquer my thoughts and try to see the positives in my situation. Life is not always easy and we all go through our struggles. I just have to know that now is my time to trust in God and strengthen my faith, to focus on him and not on myself or slip into having a pity party.

Sorry for unloading all of this on you. This is just a small bit of what is going on.

My heart went out to my friend as she struggled in the midst of her difficulties to make sense out of her life. We all want to know why trials come our way.

God alone holds the answer to the age-old mystery of suffering. Faith allows us to accept that some of our deepest questions will remain unanswered, at least for a season. There are some tragedies we will never understand until we see the other side of eternity. Sometimes we have to trust God even though we don't know how or when He is going to accomplish what needs to be done. The one thing we can know is that God is aware of and concerned about our problems. Our heartaches are precious to Him, and He has great purpose in our suffering.

Let's briefly review some of God's amazing attributes and consider a few more. The Bible tells us that God is sovereign and omnipotent over all His creation. His wisdom and knowledge are infinite, and His goodness, mercy, and grace are boundless. God is love; His compassion will never cease, and His faithfulness will endure forever. His righteousness and justice know no ends, and He is Holy and pure beyond all measure. He is the same yesterday, today, and forever. He is Truth, and His Word is Truth. In short, God is perfect in power, virtue, knowledge, and understanding. If you are willing to accept these truths about God, then take heart; God is up to something good even in the darkest places of your grief.

Your trial did not surprise God. There are no random events. God ordained all the days of your life (Psalm 139:16), and that includes your bad days. Failing to acknowledge God's sovereignty will leave you to fend for yourself in an insecure world, where evil seems out of control. It will rob you of the comfort of knowing that God is purposefully working your trials for your ultimate good. It will lead you to the inconsolable conclusion that the agony you are experiencing is meaningless and unredeemable.

We can cry, complain, and shake our fists at God. There comes a time when we have to lay aside our bitterness, anger, and despair and simply confess, "I don't understand, but I chose to trust God in this." The choice is ours. If we refuse to do so, we will never move beyond our pain, nor will we experience victory. The Bible is clear: in the midst of our suffering God stands ready to bless us with hope, encouragement, strength, wisdom, and, yes, even joy.

I find the relationship of suffering and joy the most curious. They are frequently coupled together in the Bible. Notice how the apostle Peter links the two when you read 1 Peter 1:3-9.

In this epistle, Peter tells us that biblical joy is grounded in the relationship we have with God through Jesus Christ. It is based on a "living hope" as we place our trust in the resurrected Christ. God's Word promises us that we can experience joy in the midst of tremendous suffering because we have confidence in two truths. First, we have an imperishable inheritance waiting for us in heaven. Second, our suffering is neither useless nor senseless. If we allow God to work in our lives, He will use our suffering to reveal a faith that has been tested and proves to be genuine and more valuable than gold!

In this chapter we will examine God's objectives in our adversities. We will delve into some biblical explanations regarding how suffering can bring us forth like gold.

Your faith will be proven genuine or spurious during times of trouble. Adversities are a valuable tool God uses to test the mettle— or should I say metal—of our faith. God's knowledge and wisdom are perfect. There are few things in life as profitable as learning to endure trials and responding appropriately to them.

Hardships:

- develop Christ-like attitudes within us (sanctification)
- build perseverance, character, and spiritual growth
- refine our faith for a future purpose
- bring out eternal hope in us
- advance the gospel
- develop compassion, equipping us to encourage others
- reveal our eternal glory
- enable us to know God and experience a closer relationship with Him
- bring praise, honor, and glory to God
- give us the opportunity to witness to the heavenly beings
- teach us dependency on God

- reveal to us what we really value

- discipline us

- humble us or prevent us from becoming proud

Let's look at some of these things in greater depth.

God's Ultimate Goal

Throughout much of my life I viewed Jesus as little more than my ticket to Heaven. I thought being "saved" was simply a matter of acknowledging Jesus and thanking Him for forgiving my sins. I figured it was up to me to live life the best I could and show up in Heaven when it was over. What a distorted view of salvation! Conversion is not the end of the good work God does in our lives; it is the beginning!

When we humbly accepted God's Grace and received Christ as our Savior, He wiped the slate clean. The Bible simply and profoundly describes the change that has occurred.

> *Therefore, if anyone is in Christ, he is a new creation; the old has gone, the new has come! (2 Corinthians 5:17)*

Amazing as this change is, God is not interested in leaving us there. The apostle Paul tells us that He has even more exciting things planned for us.

> *Being confident of this, that he who began a good work in you will carry it on to completion until the day of Christ Jesus. (Philippians 1:6)*

So what is this "good work," and what is its completion? Paul answers these questions in his letter to the Thessalonians. Find out for yourself in 1 Thessalonians 4:1-3.

According to the apostle Paul we are to live a life that pleases God. But there is more to it than that. This God-pleasing lifestyle is a process, not an event. We should increasingly strive to do His *will* by allowing God to *sanctify* us.

The English word *sanctified* is derived from the Greek root *hagios* (adjective), which means *holy* or *separated*. In this context it means being set apart from sexual impurity; however, the general meaning of *holy* refers to being *set apart from* all that is unclean and being *consecrated to* the Divine (Romans 12:1-2).

Sanctification is the process whereby God takes sinful people and makes them holy. This is the "good work" referred to in Philippians 1:6. God sets us apart from the sinful world around us and makes us more Christ-like. Many of us remember the following passage:

And we know that in all things God works for the good of those who love him, who have been called according to his purpose. (Romans 8:28).

We want to cling to the comforting promise that God uses every life event (even suffering, temptation, and sin) for our temporal and eternal welfare. Most Christians are not as familiar with the verse immediately following; yet it is at the very heart of this reassuring promise:

*For those God foreknew he also predestined to be **conformed to the likeness of his Son,** that he might be the firstborn among many brothers. (Romans 8:29)*

Did you get that? God's ultimate purpose in working "all (*good and bad*) things together" is to make us like His beloved Son, Jesus Christ.

John, in his first epistle, wrote something similar.

Dear friends, now we are children of God, and what we will be has not yet been made known. But we know that when he appears, we shall be like him, for we shall see him as he is. Everyone who has this hope in him purifies himself, just as he is pure. (1 John 3:2-3)

The English words *purifies* and *pure* come from the same Greek root that we studied earlier: *hagios.*

The Christian life is a process of becoming more and more like Christ. This is a life-long process that will not be complete until we go home to be with the Lord. The knowledge that our ultimate destiny is Christ-like perfection should inspire us to keep ourselves morally straight.

Do not be confused by the terminology "purifies himself." Scripture affirms that God is the One who purifies us, but as these verses suggest, we bear responsibility too; we are to act consistently with our calling. The action we must take in order to remain morally healthy is to "live by the Spirit." In other words, we must allow the Holy Spirit to reign in our lives (Galatians 5:16).

So there's God's bottom line—to make you more like Christ! If you get this into your thinking, it will clear up a lot of confusion for you. The next time disappointments and heartaches occur, understand that God is sculpting you into the image of His Son. Like an expert stone cutter, He is holding the hammer and chisel to your life, and sometimes the grooves He cuts are deep and painful! Contrary to what millions in our affluent society choose to believe, God is not trying to make us happy; He is trying to make us holy. He does not pamper us with His love; He perfects us. If we allow God to work in our lives, He will use our suffering to create within us Christ-like character.

Spiritual Maturity

> *Consider it pure joy, my brothers, whenever you face trials of many kinds, because you know that the testing of your faith develops perseverance. Perseverance must finish its work so that you may be mature and complete, not lacking anything. (James 1:2-4)*

> *Not only so, but we also rejoice in our sufferings, because we know that suffering produces perseverance; perseverance, character; and character, hope. And hope does not disappoint us, because God has poured out his love into our hearts by the Holy Spirit, whom he has given us. (Romans 5:3-5)*

Consider it pure joy whenever you face trials. Rejoice in our sufferings. What on earth are James and Paul saying? Does God really expect us to jump for joy every time tragedy strikes? Over the next several pages, let's look closely at these verses to see what they really mean.

A joyful attitude in the midst of struggles doesn't come easily—even to spiritually mature Christians. The word *consider* is the key. It signifies a deliberate and careful judgment not based on subjective feelings. This means that when painful circumstances invade our lives we are not to react. Instead, we are to make a conscious effort to "consider" carefully the future blessings that those hardships will have in our lives if we respond favorably to them. Biblical joy in times of sorrow is not mere optimism. There will be anguish and tears, but at a deeper level there will be a quiet confidence from knowing that God is in control.

A trial may come upon us unexpectedly, but trials in general should not surprise us. Both passages treat trials as an expected, normal part of life. We get into trouble when we think that wholesome, Christian living will spare us from trials. When adversity hits we are left confused and angry, wondering what we did wrong or why God failed to protect us. Adversity is not necessarily the result of "bad behavior." The last thing we need to do when we are suffering is add false guilt to our pain.

There are several things we are to experientially know about suffering and hardship.

- God is using this trial to strengthen and test our faith.

- Trials are used by God to produce perseverance.

- Perseverance develops good character and spiritual maturity.

- These virtues in turn instill unfailing hope within us.

- God's love is present with us in our trials through the Holy Spirit.

I must add a word of warning! While God gives us everything we need to come through the "testing" with perseverance and increased faith, we can choose to not consider, we can decide not to persevere. We can respond foolishly and allow suffering to weaken our faith by using it as an excuse to become bitter, miserable, and self-focused.

A Lesson from the Trees

A landscaper-friend told me a story about an incident that occurred at Biosphere 2, near Tucson, Arizona. The 3.15-acre facility consists of skylights, underground water sources, perpetual electricity, vegetable gardens, aquariums, plants, and plenty of oxygen-replenishing trees. This amazing structure was constructed as a self-sustaining, enclosed biological laboratory allowing scientists to monitor the ever-changing chemistry of its air, water, and soil.

It wasn't long before an interesting dilemma was observed. The trees planted inside Biosphere 2 remained weak and would not stay upright beyond one year. The researchers studied the soil, water source, and fertilizers, but they were unable to determine why the trees remained weak. An arborist was called in to examine the situation. After a short while he concluded that the trees would never maintain adult life without the wind—a feature that was totally absent in this closed-system laboratory. The wind causes a young tree's roots to reach down deep, thus stabilizing the tree. This daily stress upon the tree results in the formation of "reaction wood," a strong cellulose substance that helps it remain in its upright position.

We are so like the trees! Without the winds of adversity our roots will never go down deep enough to keep us standing strong as adults. The difficult seasons in our life should develop character and resilience to the storms that we will all experience!

Faith Tested by Fire

God allows trials because He wants to refine and perfect us like precious metals. This analogy is used throughout the Old and New Testaments. Take a look at Isaiah 48:10 and Job 23:8-10.

God allows trials into our lives *not* because He is displeased with us, but because He is refining us for a future purpose. He wants us to be an instrument that He can use to affect humanity; but understand that God uses no one until He tests him first. The biblical accounts tell us that Christ was led into the desert by the Holy Spirit to be tempted by Satan for forty days. After successfully passing His tests, Christ's miracle ministry began. If that applies to God's Son, it surely applies to us.

It is vital that we endure our trials while holding on to the promises of God.

The manner in which we respond while undergoing trials determines the level that God can use us. It also determines how long we stay in the fire of testing. By responding wrongly to adversity, it can drag on for years or even a lifetime. As the Israelites discovered (Numbers

13–14), problems do not have to be permanent unless we develop a rebellious attitude that refuses to submit to the will of God.

Be encouraged! God always goes into the fire with you (Isaiah 43:2; Daniel 3:8-30), and He is able and willing to deliver you from it at the proper time. When you "come forth as gold" you will enter a new season of rest.

Perseverance—Waiting on God's Timing

The apostles James and Paul want us to know that trials develop *perseverance* within us. This word is translated from the Greek noun *hypomonē*. It signifies a patient steadfast waiting and the ability to bear up bravely and calmly under misfortunes by holding fast to one's faith in Christ.

When hardships come one of the first things we want to do is get out from under them. Typically we ask God to take the suffering away from us because it is painful and unbearable. But God is trying to produce staying power in us so that we can remain brave throughout our trial. According to author and pastor James MacDonald:

> Staying power is the funnel through which all Christian virtue flows. There is nothing good that God brings into your life by way of transformation that He doesn't bring through the funnel of perseverance. … God can get every characteristic of Christ into your life if He can just teach you to persevere.[1]

God uses issues of timing to stretch our faith. We will never become spiritually mature until we learn to wait for what we want while enduring the thing we do not want. Patient endurance brings peace and joy into any situation and is a powerful witness to unbelievers. If waiting brings us frustration, it will create major stress that will ruin our enjoyment of life. When we learn to value those times of waiting, God will faithfully go to work for us.

Sometimes His delay allows us time to exhaust all other avenues of help. He waits until we realize that we are helpless without Him—that our situation is so hopeless, so bleak that if He doesn't help us, there will be no other help. Sometimes God makes us wait until we are ready to receive His blessing. Maturity takes time. We may not be ready to bring our minds, wills, and emotions in line with His will, or we may not have enough wisdom to correctly handle the thing God wants to give us.

God has a unique plan for our lives, but He also has a corporate plan for the world. Sometimes our prayer cannot be answered until God works something out with other people. God does not manipulate human beings like chess pieces. He lovingly guides and prompts them. When we are waiting for something that involves other people, we have to realize they may not be ready.

Adopting a submissive attitude does not mean that we should passively endure our situation without praying for relief, nor does it imply that we shouldn't take godly steps to remedy the problem. For example, if you have lost your job, it is right to pray for wisdom and direction while seeking employment. A submissive attitude means persevering and withstanding the pressure of the trial until God removes it at His appointed time.

Character and Hope

Trials develop perseverance, which in turn strengthens our character, deepens our trust in God, and gives us greater confidence about the future. This is the pattern of Christian growth (sanctification); one virtue builds upon another as we grow in the likeness of Jesus.

I would rather possess these virtues apart from tribulation, but that isn't God's model for growth. The very definition of *character*, from the Greek *dokime*, denotes a good reputation that has been tested and proved acceptable. As applied to the New Testament, it refers to Christian virtues that have been proven through long difficult trials.

When we patiently endure trials by faith, our faith becomes stronger for the next adversity. We know through experience that we can endure because we have done it before. In this manner we will become spiritually mature and well-equipped for the purpose that God created us. The fruit of the Spirit (Galatians 5:22-23) will be evident in our daily lives. These qualities in turn produce a stable and godly character.

Hope is based on the evidence of what God has already accomplished. What He has done in the past He can and will do for us today. We can be confident that He will see us through our trials. We are to place our hope in God, not in our circumstances changing. God will never withhold blessing without purpose.

We are assured that this hope will not disappoint us, because God has proven His intention to complete His good work in us. Proof is the outpouring of God's love through the Holy Spirit.

A Beautiful Life

Maggie was a sweet, sensitive child who had a real heart for Jesus. As long as she could remember Maggie wanted a husband and two children, a boy and a girl. As a child she enjoyed playing house with her friends. The girls would line up all of their dolls in an orderly fashion as Maggie eagerly taught everyone about Jesus.

In her teenage years Maggie began to experience the normal hormonal changes. She made a firm decision, however, to remain pure until marriage. While it hurt to be teased by her classmates for being a "prude," Maggie knew she was making a wise decision by honoring God with her body, mind, and spirit. Maggie dated some in college, but she did not find anyone who seriously interested her.

The years passed, and Maggie remained single. She had a bright mind; she did well in her profession as a physical therapist and had the respect of both clients and colleagues. Maggie had a close family, a wonderful Christian support system, and a strong relationship with the Lord, yet deep inside she hurt because her longing for a husband and children remained elusive.

Daily she prayed with fervor that God would send her His choice for a mate, but year after year her prayers went "unanswered." More than once she left a wedding reception fighting back tears of longing. Nevertheless she persevered through the difficult times and kept her focus upon God. She knew that God had a great design on her life, and she remained joyful and hopeful in her relationship with Him.

Shortly after her thirty-sixth birthday she met a gentle, kind man at work whom she grew enormously attracted to. He also took great interest in her. She knew he was not a Christian and prayed fervently for his salvation. On dates she would tell him of her love for the Lord and likewise encouraged him to share his thoughts about God. After a while, it became apparent that he simply was not interested in becoming a Christian. She despaired greatly, for she had fallen for a man who in most other aspects was what she longed for in a husband, and he loved her as well. She struggled greatly with her emotions. She longed for intimacy with him; she longed to marry him, but she knew that acting on either desire would be wrong. Telling him that she could no longer see him nearly tore her apart, but she knew that being married to a nonbeliever would only stifle her relationship with God.

The next several years were hard for Maggie. Her dreams of ever having a husband and children were growing dim. Yet she resolved to stay focused on what the Lord had for her in the present. In her greatest act of obedience, she gave her cherished dream over to the Lord to hold indefinitely for her. She resolved that if having children was not in her future, she would give love, hope, and the knowledge of Jesus to children some other way.

Through her church she volunteered at the children's hospital, where she was assigned to work twice a week with Pastor Mike, the hospital chaplain. Maggie felt very fulfilled around the children. She and Pastor

Mike shared their love for the Lord with the little ones as well as with each other in the hospital cafeteria.

Several months later something wonderful happened: they began to realize their love for each other. Two hearts that were devoted to the Lord and had longed for a family had finally found each other. Two weeks before her thirty-ninth birthday, Maggie and Mike married. Thirteen months later Maggie gave birth to twins, a boy and a girl. She and Mike lovingly began teaching their children, Thom and Cassie, about Jesus.

Through her years of waiting Maggie bravely bore her unfulfilled longings by holding firm to her faith in Christ. Was her patient, steadfast devotion to the Lord worth it? Maggie states it this way: "Serving the Lord together with Mike has turned out to be more fulfilling and meaningful than anything I could have ever dreamed. The Lord is at the center of our lives and holds the two of us tightly together through the ups and downs of life. We also have a close, loving relationship with Thom and Cassie. Together we have given many parents and their children hope through faith in Christ. Through the years I held tightly on to my dream," Maggie continues, "but when I finally gave it over to God, He took it and made something much more beautiful out of it."

Advancing the Gospel

Affliction and persecution sometimes serve to advance the kingdom of God, as we see in Acts. "On that day a great persecution broke out against the church at Jerusalem, and all except the apostles were scattered throughout Judea and Samaria. …Those who had been scattered preached the word wherever they went" (Acts 8:1, 4).

When Paul wrote the book of Philippians he was imprisoned for preaching the gospel. Rather than becoming angry and bitter with God, Paul saw his imprisonment as an opportunity to advance the gospel, as we see in Philippians 1:12-14. Through his letters he encouraged believers who were afraid of persecution. Inside the confines of the prison, Paul reached out to his captors.

What are the difficult circumstances in your life? Are you facing a financial catastrophe? Do you have a serious illness, or are you struggling with some kind of family crisis? How you respond in adversity will clearly tell others what you really believe. Rather than responding in fear and anxiety, try to find a way to demonstrate your faith. Whether or not the situation improves, your faith will grow stronger and, quite possibly, so will the faith of those observing you!

Bringing Comfort to Others

Scripture implores us to be gentle with one another. Suffering develops within us a deeper sense of mercy, empathy, and compassion. It prepares us for a future ministry to others who are also suffering. But first we must allow God to heal us. A person who can't feel pain or an individual who is unable to heal from emotional wounds tends to hurt other people either deliberately or inadvertently.

Do you have a tender, kind, compassionate heart? Do you empathize with others in their distress? If so, then you can probably remember back to a time of similar suffering. Don't despise the affliction you have gone through or the anguish you may be experiencing. Ask God to heal you so you can be a blessing to others (2 Corinthians 1:3-7).

Many wonderful ministries aimed at helping people during their personal tragedies were founded by individuals who survived the very crisis that they are now helping others overcome.

To Know God

Suffering enables us to know God in a deeper more intimate way.

My ears had heard of you but now my eyes have seen you.
(Job 42:5)

Are you familiar with the story of Job? He was a wealthy and upright man who suddenly lost his possessions, his children, his servants, and his health. The only things not taken from him were his discouraging wife and friends! He did not understand why he was suffering. Job's friends were anything but comforting. Wrongly assuming that all afflictions came as a result of one's personal sin, they tried to convince Job to repent. Job vehemently maintained his innocence and refused to takes his wife's advice to "curse God and die."

Through his ordeal Job continued to trust in God saying, "The LORD gave and the LORD has taken away; may the name of the LORD be praised" (Job 1:20).

The thing that troubled Job the most was not knowing why God had allowed these tragedies to occur. He begged God to explain His actions. Yet, day after day, while his friends continued to berate him, God remained silent. Finally, in all His glory, power, and majesty, God spoke out of a mighty storm and confronted Job. Rather than explaining, God let Job know—in no uncertain terms—that He is in complete control of the world, that He alone is capable of understanding the workings of the physical and moral universe, and that He is not obliged to explain to mortals why He allows righteous people to suffer.

Although Job's questions were left unanswered, he was awestruck by God's glorious presence, and this was more than enough for Job. He was completely satisfied with this mysterious nonanswer and fell in humble reverence before God.

Job experientially learned something in his awesome encounter with God: When nothing else is left, God will always be there, and that is more than enough. Any issue of trust suddenly evaporated. As righteous and faithful as Job had been all his life, he had never grasped so acutely the majesty, sovereignty, and immensity of God as he did on the day he finally saw God through the "eyes" of faith. Everything else fell into insignificance.

The apostle Paul also knew what it was like to suffer. In 2 Corinthians 11:16-33, he gives a detailed account of the suffering that he endured for Christ. Yet in his prison letter to the Philippians he makes this amazing statement:

> *But whatever was to my profit I now consider loss for the sake*
> *of Christ. What is more, I consider everything a loss compared*
> *to the surpassing greatness of knowing Christ Jesus my Lord,*
> *for whose sake I have lost all things. I consider them rubbish,*
> *that I may gain Christ. (Philippians 3:7-9)*

Paul used the Greek word *gnosis*, which means more than mere head knowledge of Christ. Paul captured the Old Testament concept of knowing God (which we studied in chapter four) and applied it to Christ. He wanted to know Christ in the same manner that a parent and child or a husband and wife would know each other—a knowledge based on personal experience and intimate relationship. Paul hungered to know Christ's character intimately.

This was so important to Paul that he joyfully accepted the loss of all other things in order to gain such a relationship with Christ. Think about it: Everything we would consider worthwhile—material benefits, status, honor, physical comfort, and so forth—Paul considered to be a total loss when compared to knowing Christ. It wasn't so much that those things were worthless, but compared to the astonishing privilege of knowing Christ Jesus, they simply faded into oblivion.

Through their sorrow and loss Job and Paul came to know the love, grace, and heart of God; they experienced wholeness to life that they had never known before.

We look at them and say, "I want what they have but I don't want to go through what they did to get it." But there are no shortcuts.

Both men unflinchingly declared, even in the midst of their affliction, that their suffering was well worth it!

Dependence on God

Suffering teaches us to trust in God. Adversity reminds us that we are helpless apart from Him. (2 Corinthians 1:8-10)

Most of us elect to be our own god and end up taking on more than we can handle. As confident and capable as we are in certain areas of life, we don't have it all together, and we never will. Every situation is susceptible to one form of disaster or another. Just when we get this thing together, something over here breaks. If we get that thing under control, something over there falls apart. Our Creator fashioned us to be dependent upon Him, and He has always promised to provide for, protect, and bless His own. God sends trials, and we tend to do everything we can to save ourselves. God wants us to come to a place where we can say, "God, if you don't rescue me, I am going to sink."

It was from personal experience that Paul wrote, "When I am weak, then I am strong" (2 Corinthians 12:10). We are strong when we realize we are helpless, when we trust in God for everything, and when we draw on His power and unlimited resources.

We learn to trust God when going through experiences that require trust. As we see God's faithfulness repeatedly demonstrated in our lives, we gradually come to a place where we let go of our self-reliance and learn to lean on God.

When we refuse to let God be the God of our lives, we will eventually crash and burn. That is a significant reason why God, in His mercy, allows us to keep struggling with problems. It causes us to rightfully look to God for consolation and support in our trials.

Self-Realization

Have you ever thought you were strong in a particular virtue, such as honesty or forgiveness, only to find yourself lying to protect yourself or responding in a vindictive manner during an anguishing trial? Me too! It hurts to discover the truth. Remember that God's objective is to develop Christ-like character within us, and He sometimes has to move us out of our self-satisfaction to do it.

Long difficult trials bring out character flaws that we didn't know existed—much as dross rises to the surface when silver or gold is heated to extreme temperatures. The way we respond to suffering reveals a lot about the strength and sincerity of our faith. During long, agonizing trials we come to discover what our values, beliefs, and priorities truly are. The first step to overcoming a character flaw is to recognize it.

The Bible tells us that the truth will set us free. This is particularly applicable to suffering. We will never be motivated to let God purge us of ungodly attitudes and behaviors as long as we think our righteousness score is an A-minus.

Discipline

There is a world of difference between a trial and a consequence of sin, and often it is not so easy to see. It is possible that God is stretching us, teaching us new truths, refining our character, or deepening our faith. It may be that we've sinned or drifted from the proper path, and sometimes we become deceived and fall into the trap of blaming others. When adversity comes it is wise to ask God to show us whether we had a part in causing the problem. If we will allow the Lord to speak to our hearts when we are wrong, suffering will teach us to appreciate and respect the work of discipline in our lives. It will help us learn to love and obey God's commandments along with His will (Job 5:17-18; Hebrews 12:10-11).

I vividly remember being smacked one time by my father for "being smart." My feelings were deeply wounded, because he completely misinterpreted the motivation and attitude behind my actions. I was often depressed as a child, but on this particular occasion I had felt happy and extroverted. There was no disrespect intended, yet my father interpreted my animated, jovial manner as such. He meant well, but in this instance my father was wrong to discipline me. I was fortunate; I had two loving parents. Although they sometimes made mistakes, they always tried to do their best in raising my brothers and me.

My heart goes out to you if you experienced abuse as a child, and I pray now that God uses your great suffering to heal you and bless you in ways you never thought possible. God often likens our relationship with Him to that of a parent and child. Unlike our earthly parents God is our perfect Parent. He never acts out of incorrect assumptions. He always knows exactly the type, intensity, and duration of the discipline needed to have its desired effect. And God never punishes someone else because of your mistakes. If someone innocently got caught in the wake of your sin, realize that their anguish also relates to the very things we have been discussing in this chapter. Be assured that God will redeem the suffering they also endured.

Pride and Arrogance

To keep me from becoming conceited because of these surpassingly great revelations, there was given me a thorn in my flesh, a messenger of Satan, to torment me. (2 Corinthians 12:7)

Scripture informs us that God sets Himself up against the proud (James 4:6, 1 Peter 5:5) and sternly warns us that those who insist on being haughty will be humbled (Proverbs 16:18, Proverbs 29:23, Isaiah 2:11-13). The Bible instructs us again and again to humble ourselves (James 4:10, 1 Peter 5:6). If we refuse God will have to step in. While the final results will be beautiful, the immediate consequences will be anything but pretty!

Suffering aimed at keeping us humble is not necessarily experienced because of arrogance on our part. The text says, "To keep me from becoming conceited." One of the things I hope you are beginning to understand is that God has an amazing plan for your life (here on earth as well as eternity). His plan for you greatly exceeds your dreams and expectations. Before you can step into your God-planned destiny, He has to prepare you for it, and He can't use a proud, arrogant person. Since He is omniscient, He knows in advance what your reaction will be to your awesome destiny. It is very tempting to conclude that our brains, good looks and amazing talent got us where we are today. To spare us from a nasty fall, God will prevent us from becoming prideful so that when we reach our destiny, we will appreciate God's part in it. The suffering God uses to keep us humble may feel like punishment, but in reality it is a blessing. Falling off a chair may be painful, but try taking a tumble off the roof and see how that feels!

Conclusion

The testing of our faith will always be a part of the human experience. God brings trials into our lives to grow our faith and to prove its authenticity. He delights in seeing us exercise our faith when we have no physical evidence to believe, and He promises to bless us when we respond to Him in faith.

Nothing kills our faith faster than reacting to adversities in an unbiblical manner. On the other hand, nothing causes our faith to flourish more than responding rightly to them. Tribulations are going to come whether or not you take these things to heart. God's Word is clear. You can experience hope and inexplicable joy in the midst of your crisis, or you can slip into self-focused despair. Which of the two states do you prefer?

Prayer Time

Father,
I know that You are sovereign over all Your creation and that
You rule with perfect wisdom and knowledge; You are righteous
and just, and Your mercy and compassion are endless. While
I usually don't understand the pain You have allowed in my
life, You have a loving purpose behind every tribulation, and
I chose to trust You. Amen.

Cultivating Your Garden of Faith

Get It Straight:

Read Romans 8:28 and answer the following:

1. What is the promise?

2. To whom is this promise guaranteed? Under what conditions?

3. Can you, as a Christian, negate this promise if you insist on maintaining a bitter, unforgiving, self-focused attitude toward your circumstances? Consider these things in your answer: Can you truly love God without trusting or obeying Him? (See John 14:1, 15, 21; John 15:5-12).

4. What does Romans 8:29 mean to you? How does this relate to Romans 8:28?

Head to Heart:

1. God uses hardships for our good. Review the ones presented in this chapter. Have you seen these at work in your life? In what way?

2. What is the world's definition of happiness? How does this contrast with biblical joy? Why can we experience joy during painful circumstances?

3. Can you think of other reasons God allows trials in our lives? Find biblical examples to back them up.

4. Instead of asking God, "Why did you allow this to happen?" what might be some better questions?

You and God:

1. Are you currently going through a trial? If so, what have you learned in this chapter that will help you deal with your struggles in a more positive way?

2. Which purposes behind suffering give you the greatest comfort and hope? Why?

3. Are there any that bother you? Why?

Scripture Memory

And we know that in all things God works for the good of those who love him, who have been called according to his purpose. For those God foreknew he also predestined to be conformed to the likeness of his Son, that he might be the firstborn among many brothers. (Romans 8:28-29)

Personal Thoughts:

_____

_____

_____

_____

_____

Chapter 7

Trusting God When Life Hurts:
(It Isn't Fair...I Didn't Do Anything Wrong!)

When I am afraid, I will trust in you.
In God, whose word I praise, in God I trust;
I will not be afraid. What can mortal man do to me?
(Psalm 56:3-4)

Healing the Wounds

One of the saddest road rage stories I ever heard occurred in the city of Phoenix. A young couple drove down the freeway on their way home. Not realizing it, the young husband cut off the car behind him. The angry driver sped up and pulled alongside the offending car while the passenger leaned out the window and fired a gun at them. The bullet hit the wife, who was five months pregnant. An ambulance rushed her to the hospital, but it was too late. Doctors tried desperately to keep the unborn child alive, but it was too young and died shortly after being delivered. At the funeral, the mother-to-be was shown in an open casket holding her tiny baby in her arms!

There are unavoidable circumstances that can throw us into a whirlwind of suffering. I am talking about the kind in which we are blameless—situations where we were innocently minding our own business and suddenly—WHAM! We feel as though we got hit between the eyes with a two-by-four that has a six-inch nail protruding out of it—and we didn't even see it coming! Perhaps the tragedy struck so early in your childhood that you don't remember life apart from "The Incident."

The injury may have been deliberate or accidental. The perpetrator may be a stranger or a loved one. He may realize the role he played in your suffering, or he may be completely ignorant of any wrongdoing. He may seek your forgiveness, or his heart may be callous and indifferent to your suffering; he may even feel justified in "getting back" at you for a past hurt he perceived was your fault. Perhaps there wasn't a person to blame; maybe it was caused by "an act of God."

Between personal experiences and the horror stories we hear on the evening news, it shouldn't be hard to come up with a list of examples:

- Betrayal
- Vicious crimes committed against you or a loved one
- Financial disasters
- Sudden tragedies
- Family problems
- Weather disasters
- Physical injuries and illnesses

When these things happen to us or to our loved ones, it is both normal and healthy to grieve. As we have seen, God promises to comfort those who turn to Him in their anguish. I pray I have given you sound reason to believe that no wound is too damaging or deep to be healed by God. Some circumstances, especially severe physical disabilities, may be with you for a lifetime. While the physical effects may be permanent, the devastation to your soul does not need to be. You can and will come through past, present, and future grief with a greater sense of peace, joy, and hope as you put your trust in Christ.

Yet if we are not careful, the pit of pain we are innocently thrust into can become a prison, and the abundant life that Christ promised us will seem little more than a fairy tale. How we react to our hurts is crucial. It determines whether our faith will flourish or flounder and whether we will heal emotionally or remain stuck in a pit of despair, bitterness, and self-pity.

Can you identify past events from which you cannot seem to heal? Many of us have at least one area of pain or disappointment from which we have yet to recover.

Tragedy and suffering are difficult for the soul to endure, but God never intended us to bear it apart from Him (Matthew 11:28-30).

When we deal with pain using our resources rather than turning to God, things tend to get ugly. The longer we dwell in our pain, the greater the risk that we will eventually move from a place of innocent suffering to a stronghold of sin. It may be our sin that is keeping us emotionally paralyzed. Even though we are innocent of the adversity that first came into our lives, the question we need to ask is, "Have I ceased to be 'innocent' in this thing?"

Nothing keeps us wallowing in the mire longer than turning to sinful behaviors for comfort within our well of misery. These behaviors can easily turn into addictions, as was the case with Margaret. She had a philandering husband who hurt her terribly. After a while she turned to alcohol for comfort and soon found herself deep in the pit of alcoholism.

Addictions may begin as a coping mechanism for pain that we were innocently pushed into.

We may also turn to sinful behaviors, because the pain inflicted upon us by others has led us to believe we are worthless. A teenager who feels unloved and unwanted by his parents may join a gang in an attempt to gain acceptance and respect. Victims of childhood sexual abuse often struggle with shame, a lack of self-respect, and feelings of worthlessness. Unable to resolve those feelings as they grow older, they sometimes turn to sinful sexual behaviors such as promiscuity and prostitution.

Chrystena, my dental assistant, relayed to me an encouraging story about her daughter's determination to deal with hurtful peers in a Christ-like way. Sixteen-year-old Allison had been having a difficult time at school. One of her classmates (whom I'll call Mary) would begin whispering to her group of friends whenever Allison came near. This apparently prompted the other girls to snicker and point, hurting Allison's feelings deeply. After several weeks she confided her painful experiences to her wise mother, who suggested that she deal with the situation by demonstrating kindness rather than anger or obvious hurt. Allison thought about this for a while; as a Christian, she did not want bitterness and negativity to dominate her thinking, so she decided to try the "sweet" approach. An opportunity came the next day while Allison was standing in the cafeteria line. Allison spotted Mary entering the cafeteria and immediately signaled for the girl to join her near the front of the line. Mary seemed a bit taken aback by the kind gesture. At the cash register, Allison topped off her good deed by offering to buy Mary some candy. Mary was visibly surprised and hesitant to accept. At Allison's insistence, however, Mary allowed Allison to treat her to a lollypop. The two girls got together later that day and worked out some of their differences.

Regardless of whether they actually become good friends, Allison did something extremely important that day. By an act of her will, Allison refused to allow anger, hurt, and other negative emotions to control her. Instead, she chose to reach out in a Christ-like way to the unfairness of her situation.

Unfortunately, my reaction to hurtful classmates was quite different. As a child I was taunted and teased about being tall. As a result I felt ugly, awkward, and undesirable. For many years I would not wear green because when I did I was called "Jolly Green Giant." I stayed in my pain long after those cruel comments ended because I chose self-pity and isolation as my companions. My life revolved around me. Although I felt worthless and inferior to others, I became extremely selfish and self-absorbed. It took an act of God to get me out.

In this fallen world life deals us cruel blows. The thing *not* to do is dwell on what others (or God) may have done to us. Before going any further I want to ask you a difficult question. Do you *want* to be healed?

I confess it took me many years to want healing for myself. Self-pity was one of my favorite emotions. I derived pleasure from parading my pain around because of the attention and sympathy I received from others. I felt insignificant, so it was comforting to elicit compassion from others. It was a way of feeling affirmed—a sign that there may be something lovable in me after all.

Sharing my pain often caused others to take sides. I enjoyed getting my audience to side with me against those who had caused me pain. It was my way of getting back at them.

There are complex reasons why people may not want to escape from their places of anguish.

Can you relate to any of these?

• The fear of change: Life may not be pleasant, but at least the sufferers have learned how to survive with the pain. Those carrying childhood hurts are especially susceptible to this mind-set.

- Pain causes its victims to become self-absorbed. They don't know how to shift their attention to others.

- They find comfort in blaming their failures and inadequacies on others. They reason that anyone in their situation would have the same shortcomings.

- They are so caught up in their emotions they can't think rationally. They don't believe change is possible.

- Instead of turning to God they use their resources to try to free themselves. This is characteristic of people who have become trapped in addictive sin.

- They are angry at God and don't want His help. If He were to rescue them, they might feel obliged to follow His ways rather than their own.

- They would rather hold on to the pain than forgive the person who caused them anguish.

Some of these attitudes and behaviors may not seem that bad, but according to God's Word, they are all sinful because they are self-focused. That is, they remove God from His rightful place in our lives and replace Him with "Self." These attitudes and behaviors express distrust, unbelief, and a deep lack of faith in God. They proclaim to God that He is unwilling or incapable of taking good care of us and that we would do better on our own. Harboring these attitudes will keep us in our place of pain indefinitely.

There are other serious impediments to healing as well.

Unforgiveness

Forgiveness does not come easily, especially on an emotional level. When we've been badly hurt, we don't *feel* like forgiving the offending person, even if she repents. At the very least we want to let her "twitch" for a while so she too knows what it feels like to hurt. More than likely we want her to pay big-time for her shameful deeds. Nevertheless, we will remain in our pain until we forgive those who had a hand in putting us there, *ourselves included.*

Jesus said the greatest commandments are to love God and to love others. If we are resentful and unforgiving, we're being disobedient. Not only does an unforgiving, bitter heart displease God, it also spreads its gangrenous infection to others. Our acidic words may well be the means by which innocent people are pulled into the pit along with us.

During His earthly ministry Jesus had a lot to say about forgiveness; the Scriptures make it clear God wants us to take the concept of forgiveness seriously! So if we want to please and obey God, we must find a way to sweep resentment out of our hearts and truly forgive those who have wronged us.

It begins by realizing that God will not put any of us through something that He was not willing to experience Himself. Forgiveness cost God the death of His beloved Son. Jesus Christ came to reconcile all of us to God, yet He was rejected and tortured to death on a Roman cross. As He hung on that cross, He asked His Father to forgive them (us). He suffered in our place so that we could be made right with God. You may never understand why you were treated wrongly. Yet Jesus does, because He suffered more than any of us.

We need to understand our correct position before God as judge over all (Romans 12:19). God is the only competent judge. He knows the thoughts and motives of every person's heart. He is the only One who has the knowledge, wisdom, and power to execute perfect justice. We must trust Him to deal rightly with each person.

We have studied a lot about God's sovereignty. Remembering that God has allowed this to happen for His purpose and our ultimate good (Romans 8:28) will go a long way toward helping us control our anger, drive out resentment, and get ready to forgive.

Forgiveness will never make what happened *to* us okay, but it does make *us* okay! Resentment and unforgiveness place us in bondage and obstruct God's blessings and abundant grace from flowing to us and through us. When we disentangle our hearts from an unforgiving spirit, we will stop emotionally dragging the offender everywhere we go, we will stop allowing the offenses of our enemies to wound us further, we will get rid of the hatred that eats away at our soul, we will enjoy restored relationships with God and others, and we will re-enter a place of peace and wholeness.

Forgiveness Exemplified

When I reflect upon amazing acts of human forgiveness, I think of Corrie ten Boom. During the Nazi occupation of Holland in World War II, she and her family became involved with the Dutch Underground. As committed Christians the ten Booms could not in good conscience look the other way while God's chosen people were being openly persecuted. They began hiding Jews in a secret room built into their home. Their one-and-a-half-year involvement with the Underground ended abruptly when the Gestapo broke into their home and dragged them off to prison. Her father died there ten days later. Corrie and her sister Betsie were later transported to Ravensbrück concentration camp where, for ten months, they suffered greatly at the hands of the Nazis. Betsie finally succumbed to illness and died there. Three days later Corrie was released due to a clerical error.

After the war ended Corrie began traveling and telling her story in order to encourage other Christians. In 1947, after she spoke to a church in Munich, Germany, a man walked up to her and extended his hand. To her horror, she recognized him as the S.S. guard who had been posted at the shower room door at the Ravensbrück processing center!

He had become a Christian; his sins had been cleansed by Christ, and now he sought Corrie's forgiveness as well. In her book *The Hiding Place*, Corrie ten Boom describes this soul shattering experience:

His hand was thrust out to shake mine. And I, who had preached so often to the people in Bloemendaal the need to forgive, kept my hand at my side.

Even as the angry, vengeful thoughts boiled through me, I saw the sin of them. Jesus Christ had died for this man; was I going to ask for more? Lord Jesus, I prayed, forgive me and help me to forgive him.

I tried to smile, I struggled to raise my hand. I could not. I felt nothing, not the slightest spark of warmth or charity. And so again I breathed a silent prayer. Jesus, I cannot forgive him. Give me Your forgiveness.

As I took his hand the most incredible thing happened. From my shoulder along my arm and through my hand a current seemed to pass from me to him, while into my heart sprang a love for this stranger that almost overwhelmed me.

And so I discovered that it is not on our forgiveness any more than on our goodness that the world's healing hinges, but on His.[1]

I have touched ever so briefly on this important subject. If you are having a difficult time forgiving someone who threw you into a place of suffering, I encourage you to seek godly counsel and read some good Christian books on this subject. Above all, I urge you to search out what the Scriptures teach and ask God to help you come to a place where you are willing to forgive.

Bitterness

It's easy to become angry when we see bad things happening to good people, but the pot of bitterness really gets stirred up when we watch good things happening to bad people, especially the bad people who hurt us. Let's get some insight into this from Scripture by reading Psalm 73.

Sometimes it appears that God turns a deaf ear to the afflicted while the guilty prosper. We, like the psalmist, often wonder why God allows bad people to attain worldly success while cursing His name. Regardless of how it appears, Scripture clearly affirms that God sees and takes note of every evil deed. He hates sin and sets Himself against those who do evil.

I love Psalm 73; it's so like me! The discouragement the psalmist is feeling has resulted because he allowed his faith to be overtaken by self-focused thinking. He became discouraged, depressed, and embittered when he contrasted the apparent prosperity of the wicked with the afflictions of the righteous. It was only when the psalmist turned to worship God ("entered the sanctuary of God") in verse 17 that he began to understand God's perspective on the fate of the wicked. As he worshiped God, his thoughts moved from self to God.

Those who reject God will perish in their sins. When we relinquish our lives to the control of our sovereign, holy God, we come to understand that it is the wicked, not the righteous, who are in trouble.

Regardless of whether or not we see the wicked come to shame in this earthly life, we must trust God. Justice is important to God, and He promises to utterly destroy unrepentant sinners that come against Him. Always remember that those who sin against you sin first and foremost against God!

Listening to Lies

When we are broken, especially by people who betrayed us, the enemy will tell us that others have thwarted our destiny and that our future is ruined. The truth is no one other than you can thwart your destiny. Even if men forget you, God will not. God in His sovereignty will use your pain as a means of delivering you to your destiny, if you let Him.

Do you know the story of Joseph? You can read about his remarkable life in Genesis 37:1–50:26. In his early years Joseph was overconfident and prideful. He flaunted his favorite-son status before his brothers along with the amazing vision God had given him regarding his destiny. One day Joseph, at his father's request, went to find his brothers, who were grazing their flocks quite a distance from home. As Joseph approached them they seized him and threw him into an empty cistern to die. Later they saw a caravan of Ishmaelites on their way to Egypt. They pulled Joseph out of the cistern and sold him to them. In Egypt, he was sold as a slave to Potiphar, unjustly thrown into prison, and forgotten. Through an odd twist of events over a thirteen-year period, Joseph became the second most powerful ruler in Egypt. He managed the nation wisely during its seven years of plenty so that it would continue to thrive through the seven-year famine. Joseph's brothers eventually came under his authority when they traveled to Egypt to buy grain.

When confronting his brothers about their evil deed, Joseph said, "You intended to harm me, but God intended it for good" (Genesis 50:20).

The very evil that Joseph's brothers used against him in an attempt to destroy his future was the very thing that God used to catapult Joseph to his great destiny.

The best place we can be is at the center of God's will, because He will take full responsibility for the outcome. Do not fall prey to the lies of the pit! Be assured that God will never allow your destiny to lie in the hands of other people.

Running to God

The way to our deliverance is to bring everything to God—and I mean *everything*! We must present to Him the whole ugly mess, all of our heartaches; brokenness; sin; failed attempts; and destructive emotions such as anger, bitterness, unforgiveness, self-pity and discouragement. If we surrender everything to Him, He can and will heal us from wounds that were inflicted upon us.

I am all for getting godly counsel, but know this: A godly adviser will always point you back to Christ as your deliverer.

The key to getting out of the pit is to call out to God. We must trust God and cry out for His help. We can turn to God in our grief because:

- He alone has the knowledge, wisdom, understanding and power to deliver us in the exact manner we need to be delivered and at the proper time. (Isaiah 40:10)

- He is sympathetic, and His compassion is endless (Lamentations 3:19-23)

- He knows our needs and our vulnerabilities, and He will never leave or forsake us. Unlike humans, God is never overwhelmed by the depth of our needs. (Psalm 88:1-4 and Psalm 9:9-10)

- He understands because He has been there. Christ was betrayed and abandoned, yet He chose to do His Father's will. Jesus went to the pit so that we could be delivered out of the pit. (Matthew 27:46)

- He understands temptation because He was tempted in every way we are. (Hebrews 4:15-16)

- He met temptation without sin. Regardless of how we responded in the past, a way does exist for us to be victorious. It is never too late to start following His example. (1 Corinthians 10:12-13)

So one final question: Are you willing to be healed on God's terms—His way instead of your own way? If so, then look up! You are already on your way up.

If you are not yet ready, then don't get discouraged and give up. Ask Him daily to bring you to the point where you are willing to trust Him fully. God has not given up on you, and He doesn't want you to either. All He asks is that you start where you are. Even if you have to pray, "Lord, I can't say I want to do it Your way, but there is something deep within me that wants to come to the place where that desire is born. Please help me!"

Prayer Time

Father,
Thank You for not giving up on me and for meeting me where I am rather than where I should be. Reveal to me what I need to bring to You and show me anything I am currently holding back. Bring me to the point where I am willing to trust You fully. I acknowledge that You alone are my healer. There is no emotional pain that is too deep or too long-standing for You to heal. I pray these things in the name of my healer and deliverer, Jesus Christ. Amen.

Cultivating Your Garden of Faith

Get It Straight:

1. Sometimes when we say verses by rote we rush over them without true understanding. Carefully read Matthew 6:12. In what manner (or by what standard) are we asking God to forgive us?

2. Read Matthew 5:21-25, 5:43-44, 6:12-14, 18:21-35. What do these passages say about forgiveness? (I encourage you to consult some good commentaries.)

3. It can be demoralizing to watch good things happen to bad people. Read 2 Peter 3:3-10. Why is God slow in bringing the wicked to justice? Aren't you glad God gave *you* time to repent!

Head to Heart:

1. What personal benefits do we reap by forgiving our adversaries? Can you think of others not discussed in this chapter?

2. When we are stuck in a mire of pain, Satan's lies are very convincing. What are some of the falsehoods he likes to throw at us?

3. Running *to* God is our only way out of the pit. We looked at six reasons why we can turn to God. Look at that bulleted list again (page 124) and contrast it with people. Why are human beings deficient in "rescuing" us?

4. As human beings, why do we sometimes find satisfaction in wallowing in misery? Can you think of other reasons we may not want to be healed?

You and God:

1. Can you identify past hurts from which you cannot seem to heal? In each case ask God to show you whether or not you have ceased to be innocent (see Psalm 139:23-24).

2. Can you identify with any of the reasons a person may not want to be healed? If so, are you willing to confess these things to God?

3. The key to getting out of the pit is to call out to God. Are you willing to be healed on God's terms? If not, what is stopping you?

🌱

Scripture Memory

"For I know the plans I have for you," declares the LORD, "plans to prosper you and not to harm you, plans to give you hope and a future." (Jeremiah 29:11)

Personal Thoughts:

_____

_____

_____

_____

_____

Chapter 8

Biblical Prosperity

Blessed are all who fear the LORD,
who walk in his ways. You will eat
the fruit of your labor; blessings and
prosperity will be yours.
(Psalm 128:1-2)

I don't like waiting in the checkout line at the grocery store. Watching someone's box of corn flakes and bag of tortilla chips move along the conveyor belt ceased to amuse me somewhere around the age of seven. While I haven't resorted to counting packs of gum displayed near the cash register, I have attempted to alleviate my boredom by sneaking a peek at the front-page tabloid headlines where the latest scandals of the rich and famous are blatantly exposed. You know the kind of stuff I am referring to: the glamour couple whose marriage is on the rocks; the actress who tried to commit suicide; the rock star who was charged with a DUI; photographs of Hollywood beauties who are either getting fat or becoming dangerously thin; the politician who got caught in a sex scandal. It seems that the gamut of human sin and sorrow is portrayed on the front page of a single tabloid.

As much as our culture tries to deny i t, fame, fortune, and worldly success do not equate to happiness; in fact, just the opposite often seems to be true. I frequently marvel at how some of the seemingly unhappiest people in the world reside in the most exclusive neighborhoods. Conversely, I know people who are not successful by the world's standards, yet their lives are filled with contentment—a sense of purpose, peace of mind, healthy relationships, and love of God.

Why is it that worldly success—defined in terms of wealth, possessions, beauty, status, power, and fame—carries with it the assumption of happiness and the good life, when more often than not it falls short of delivering even a modest amount of joy or contentment?

Worldly Prosperity vs. Biblical Prosperity

How does the Bible's definition of success differ from that of the world? What do the Scriptures say about blessing and prosperity? What promises are given, to whom, and under what conditions?

In trying to answer these questions, we need to stop trying to put God into a neatly defined box. Consider what the New Testament asserts about eternal vs. earthly wealth as you read 1 Timothy 6:6-10.

According to these verses, true acquisition (gain) is found in godliness and contentment, whereas the *love of* money drives us to unhealthy obsessions and destructive behaviors that wreak havoc in our lives. Jesus told us, "Watch out! Be on your guard against all kinds of greed" (Luke 12:15).

Those who pursue wealth because they think it is the key to happiness miss God's true blessings, which are based on eternal riches that cannot be lost under any circumstances (Matthew 6:19-24).

The desire for riches is often a snare, because wealth can easily interfere with our instinctive need for God. When one's basic physical needs are more than adequately met, it is easy to feel smug and self-sufficient. Instead of trusting in God, the rich are tempted to trust in their money. God created each of us with an inner need for Him, and no matter how hard we try to mask that longing, it will always surface as a sense of emptiness and discontent.

Blaise Pascal, the seventeenth-century French philosopher and mathematician, expressed it this way: "There is a God shaped vacuum in the heart of every man which cannot be filled by any created thing, but only by God, the Creator, made known through Jesus."[1] If a wealthy man, who is poor toward God, feels empty inside, he can buy elaborate and exciting "toys" that, for a short time, will dull the very pain meant to drive him to God. When the excitement wears off he can indefinitely seek other adventures for that fleeting and elusive sense of fulfillment. Eventually his abundance and self-sufficiency will become a cruel and relentless master over him, and he will find himself in bondage as literally as any slave who ever existed.

Don't misunderstand—God is not opposed to riches, possessions, or any other aspect of worldly success, nor is he advocating poverty or a redistribution of wealth. Admittedly, the Bible sometimes associates the poor with righteousness and humility while the rich are occasionally portrayed as greedy, arrogant, and selfish—such as is revealed in the story of the rich man and Lazarus (Luke 16:19-31). It would be erroneous to assume that the Bible automatically classifies the poor as being virtuous and the rich as being wicked. In fact, there are many passages to the contrary.

Wealth may be a sign of God's blessing. Many of God's devoted servants such as Abraham, Job, and David were extremely wealthy men. God blessed Solomon with riches and honor as a reward because he asked God for the discernment to rule wisely over Israel (1 Kings 3:4-13). In Luke 8:3, we learn that Jesus' ministry was supported by wealthy women.

Conversely, poverty sometimes results from sin or laziness, as is indicated by the following proverb: "Lazy hands make a man poor, but diligent hands bring wealth" (Proverbs 10:4).

While the Bible shows that poverty as well as riches can be a blessing or a curse, the real question at hand is not are you wealthy or poor in a worldly sense, but are you rich or poor toward God?

Buying into the world's ideas of success is a tremendous faith-killer regardless of your financial status. The Bible wisely warns us to protect our hearts and minds from deceptive worldly thinking (Colossians 2:80).

My friend Don is not successful in a worldly sense. Although he was extremely well educated, he was never able to become well-established in his field of expertise or earn the kind of money others in his profession did. To make matters worse, his wife earned a lot more money than he did. Comparing himself with his wife and peers only caused Don to berate himself. He allowed shallow external values to dominate his thinking and crush his spirit. He has since divorced and has retreated into a rather mundane existence. Feeling neglected by God, Don struggles with a deep sense of disappointment—even resentment—toward God because he never "made it" in life.

Consider the following verses from the book of James:

> *The brother in humble circumstances ought to take pride in his high position. But the one who is rich should take pride in his low position, because he will pass away like a wild flower. For the sun rises with scorching heat and withers the plant; its blossom falls and its beauty is destroyed. In the same way, the rich man will fade away even while he goes about his business. (James 1:9-11)*

These verses are meant to bring balance to the attitude of both rich and poor. The poor man may use his poverty as an excuse to become despairing, bitter, lazy, or covetous. It may cause him to give up hope, or it may lure him into an unhealthy obsession with obtaining money. Because of his poverty, like my friend Don, he may feel neglected, unworthy, or abandoned by God. James tells this brother that in God's eyes he is loved and valued deeply. He is encouraged to focus his attention on the rich spiritual blessings that are his in Christ.

The rich man may be tempted to take pride in his wealth, prestige, and influence that has resulted from his financial success. James tells him to take pride as a believer in his humility before God. He reminds the wealthy brother that his riches are transitory in nature and will some day be gone. The rich should be thankful that money, power, and status mean nothing to God since they can be so easily lost.

James implores both the wealthy and the poor to adopt God's eternal perspective regarding poverty and riches, which comes from developing one's spiritual life, not one's financial assets.

Biblical Blessings

Biblical prosperity is difficult to define. It encompasses much more than anything we can comprehend or even imagine, for it is conceived in the very mind of God.

Although many believers enjoy material prosperity, many others live in hardship. Wealth is not necessarily a sign of faith or favoritism on God's part. Jesus said, "A man's life does not consist in the abundance of his possessions" (Luke 12:15). If earthly riches were a meaningful goal, surely Jesus would have pursued them. Instead, He chose a life where He had no place to lay His head (Matthew 8:20).

I want to re-emphasize that I am not demonizing wealth. The Lord may very well decide to bless you with earthly riches. When God brings you wealth, He will never send you off on an obsessive, compulsive journey that may cost you your family, friends, reputation, health, or right standing with Him.

The blessing of the LORD brings wealth, and he adds no trouble to it. (Proverbs 10:22)

So if biblical prosperity does not necessarily refer to worldly success, what does it refer to?

Robert Morris, in his book *The Blessed Life*, describes prosperity (or blessedness) as follows: "The days of the blessed person are filled with divine 'coincidences' and heavenly meaning. A blessed man may or may not be wealthy by the world's standards, but he enjoys a quality of life that most billionaires would envy."[2]

Beth Moore articulates biblical blessing as such: "Blessing is defined by neither ease nor worldly possessions. Blessing is bowing down to receive the expressions of divine favor that in the inner recesses of the human heart and mind make life worth the bother."[3]

After reading the previous chapters on adversity, I hope you have come to realize that biblical blessing does *not* mean the absence of hardship. Blessing and prosperity come as we place our trust in God, knowing that He will give us everything we need to triumph over our trials. As we have already learned, God desires to bless us by giving us a supernatural ability to endure our suffering so that we will remain steadfast and secure. This aspect of prosperity assures us that rather than being undone by calamity we are strengthened by it. As a result, we cultivate our faith, growing more Christ-like.

When the storm has swept by, the wicked are gone, but the righteous stand firm forever. (Proverbs 10:25)

Several years ago my friend Kaydee went on a missionary stint to the slums of Nairobi, Kenya, where she helped out at SODA (Support Orphans and Destitute Academy). The school was started by a couple who felt blessed by the Lord to own and operate two hair salons that are meager at best, at least by Western standards.

As they grew successful, instead of moving out from among these poorest of poor, Doreen and Zakayo decided to stay and run SODA where orphans, children of AIDS victims, and the truly destitute could be schooled and fed.

While there, Kaydee met brothers and sisters who lived in deplorable conditions, yet their eyes sparkled with an indescribable joy and love for the Lord. Their Bibles were well-worn, and their church was always full. As she worshiped with these precious believers her heart was deeply moved, for they joyfully praised God with an intensity that would put most of us to shame. Were these people blessed in a worldly sense? Hardly! Yet they had spiritual blessings that surpassed anything the world has to offer.

God promises to remain close to us throughout our trials. As we love Him, acknowledge Him, and call out to Him, we reap many benefits.

> *"Because he loves me," says the LORD, "I will rescue him;*
> *I will protect him, for he acknowledges my name.*
> *He will call upon me, and I will answer him;*
> *I will be with him in trouble,*
> *I will deliver him and honor him." (Psalm 91:14-15)*

When we call out to Him, He makes Himself known to us in personal and tangible ways. As we acknowledge Him, He gives us a much-needed thrust in the right direction.

Biblical prosperity is succeeding in what God has called us to do. It is the miraculous grace of God that reveals His willingness to aid us in every circumstance of life, be it hardship or ease. Biblical prosperity overflows in us and through us when we abide in Christ. As we seek Him first and ask for His blessings, His incredible grace works in every area of our lives—health, relationships, work, rest, family, emotions, thoughts, accomplishments, etc. The world can't hold a flame to this kind of prosperity!

⚘

In spite of being unjustly thrown into a pit by his brothers and sold to the Ishmaelites, Joseph firmly held on to his faith in God. He is described as prosperous and successful both as a slave in Potiphar's house and later as a prisoner. I wonder how many of us would consider ourselves prosperous and successful in such circumstances! In the biblical account, prosperity is attributed to the presence of the LORD (Genesis 39:1-23).

What an awesome testimony! Unbelievers not only recognized the presence of God in Joseph's life; they realized that they were prospering because of Joseph.

The Keys to Biblical Prosperity

While the key to success and prosperity is the manifest presence of the Lord, *obedience* and *faith* play a major role here as well. Observe how the presence of the Lord relates to obedience.

> *The LORD **was with Jehoshaphat** because in his early years he walked in the ways his father David had followed. He did not consult the Baals but sought the God of his father and **followed his commands** rather than the practices of Israel.*
> *(2 Chronicles 17:3-4)*

Conversely, the manifest presence of the Lord did not remain on those who defied Him. Time and again Saul, the first king of Israel, disobeyed the Lord. Finally, God rejected Saul as King and removed His Spirit from him. (1 Samuel 15:23, 18:12)

Throughout the Old and New Testaments, the Bible promises blessing, abundance, and prosperity for those who are obedient and put their faith in God. Here are a few examples:

• Joshua 1:7-9
• Psalm 1:1-3
• John 13:17

Please understand that obedience does not equate to legalism. Legalistic people may look good on the outside, but inside they are full of contradictions. Such Christians attempt to conform to a code of conduct that goes beyond the precepts of the Bible, and then they get caught up in judging others for how well they keep these man-made rules. Legalism is a stifling, oppressive environment where real heart change becomes impossible. The sinful patterns that God wants to weed out of their lives are only forced under the surface. They will pop up in one form or another the minute they relax their guard, come under stress, or are in a place where no one can observe them. Rules by themselves cause a person to rebel against God. This is the sad truth that Paul wrote about in Romans 7:5. Yet the strongest admonitions Christ uttered were addressed to the legalistic Pharisees.

> *"Woe to you, teachers of the law and Pharisees, you hypocrites! You are like whitewashed tombs, which look beautiful on the outside but on the inside are full of dead men's bones and everything unclean." (Matthew 23:27)*

When you're trapped in legalism, you hide behind external behaviors while deceiving yourself into believing you are closer to God. With God, motive and attitude is everything. Jesus died so we could experience genuine intimacy with Him. Because legalism prefers works over relationship, such intimacy is impossible.

This being the case, are the rules that God lays down bad? The apostle Paul emphatically answers this question: *"Certainly not!"* (Romans 7:7). If we are consumed with keeping rules, we will be worse off, because rules by themselves have no power to change us. Furthermore, Satan will have a heyday as we wallow in our failure.

Obedience is a far cry from legalism. It is born of a heart that longs for the things of God, as I encourage you to see in Psalm 119:14-16, 92-93, 127-128, 137-138, 160, and 176.

Do you see the longing to obey God in these verses? Obedience is not legalistic works; it is a heart thing! The psalmist trusts that God's commands are righteous, trustworthy, and true. While he does not obey God's laws perfectly, he is consistent. He delights in obeying the law because he has deep faith in and love for the Lawgiver!

Like the psalmist we must learn to accept that God has the sovereign right to reign in our lives. We must believe in our hearts that His rules are righteous. God is not simply trying to assert His authority over us. He loves us in ways that we can't even begin to understand. Therefore, when He sets down laws for us to follow we must trust that they are for our physical, emotional, and spiritual wellbeing. Until we internalize these beliefs we will always have an authority problem!

Christ is our perfect example. While He was here on earth, He subjected himself completely to His father's will. "My food," said Jesus, "is to do the will of him who sent me and to finish his work" (John 4:34). If Christ, "who, being in very nature God" chose to depend upon His Father, can we do any less (Philippians 2:3-13)?

While we may never see earthly rewards for obedience, the Scriptures assure us that those who obey God will be blessed.

God asks us to trust Him. If we do not reach out in faith by making a simple decision to obey Him, we will never realize that He is trustworthy. Blessing is given to those who trust in the Lord. It is the reward, satisfaction, and fulfillment that come from seeking hard after God and joyfully finding Him, as Jesus promises in His most famous sermon: "Blessed are those who hunger and thirst for righteousness, for they will be *filled*. ... *Blessed* are the pure in heart, for they will *see God*." (Matthew 5:6, 8)

Prosperity and blessedness will be a reality as we learn to love, trust, and obey the Lord, but we need more than a strong determination and self-effort to be victorious over sin and temptation. On the eve of His crucifixion Jesus told His disciples:

*"If you love me, you will obey what I command. And I will ask
the Father and he will give you another Counselor to be with you
forever—the Spirit of truth." (John 14:15-17)*

Obedience may start with our wills, but it can't stay there, because in
the end you and I will do what—deep down inside of us—we really
want to do (Romans 7:14-24). We are able to be obedient to God only
as we depend daily upon the Holy Spirit to guide us. As we do, He releases
His sanctifying power in our lives (Romans 8:5-9; Galatians 5:16).

If we yield ourselves to Him, *our* wants will slowly change to *His*
wants, and our struggle to obey Him will be a thing of the past.

*Don't copy the behavior and customs of this world, but let God
transform you into a new person by changing the way you think.
Then you will learn to know God's will for you, which is good and
pleasing and perfect." (Romans 12:2 NLT)*

When we walk closely with the Lord on a daily basis, we gain access
to His amazing wisdom, knowledge, and understanding (1 Corinthians
2:6-16). This gives us the ability to respond wisely and obediently to
the challenges of life. I have discovered how easy it is to end up on a
dead-end path by basing my thinking on mere human understanding
and reasoning. The flesh can't solve the problem because the flesh *is*
the problem!

Scripture is clear: If we choose to distrust God and disobey Him,
things will not go well with us. Yes, we may become successful by the
world's standards, but by God's standards we will be, well…I don't
think I can express it any better than Christ did many centuries ago:

*"You say, 'I am rich; I have acquired wealth and do not need
a thing.' But you do not realize that you are wretched, pitiful,
poor, blind and naked." (Revelation 3:17)*

Prosperity, Good Works, and Faith

How does biblical prosperity (blessing) and fruit (good works) relate, and what does faith have to do with it? As we studied in Chapter 4, God created us to do good works. God blesses us so that we will be a blessing to others.

Prayer plays a major role in this process, for "the prayer of a righteous man is powerful and effective" (James 5:16). As you read the amazing blessings given us through prayer, observe the conditions and the purposes associated with them.

"And I will do whatever you ask in my name, so that the Son may bring glory to the Father. You may ask me for anything in my name, and I will do it." (John 14:13-14)

"If you remain in me and my words remain in you, ask whatever you wish, and it will be given you. This is to my Father's glory, that you bear much fruit, showing yourselves to be my disciples." (John 15:7-8)

"You did not choose me, but I chose you and appointed you to go and bear fruit—fruit that will last. Then the Father will give you whatever you ask in my name." (John 15:16)

This is the confidence we have in approaching God: that if we ask anything according to his will, he hears us. And if we know that he hears us—whatever we ask—we know that we have what we asked of him. (1 John 5:14-15)

These are important, so let's go over them together:

- **The promises:** Christ will do whatever you ask; you may ask God for anything and it will be given you; you can have confidence in approaching God; the Father hears you.

- **The conditions:** you have to ask God for it; you have to ask it in Jesus' name; you must remain in Jesus and let His words remain in you (live in obedience and dependency upon Christ); you must ask according to His will; you must know that He hears you (faith);

- **The purposes:** so that the Son will bring glory to the Father; in order for the Father to be glorified; so that you will bear much fruit—fruit that will last; to fulfill what God has chosen and appointed for you to do; so that you will show yourself to be His follower (i.e., putting into practice that which you learn from Him).

In order for our prayers to be heard and answered by God, we are expected to pray in Jesus' name. Jesus invites us to pray using His authority as we ask the Father to act upon our prayers. We may confidently approach the Father because we come in the name of His beloved Son, Jesus. There is more to it than that, for adding Christ's name to the end of a prayer is not a magic formula for getting whatever we want! Carefully re-read the passages above and you will see by their context how unbiblical such a view point is. Praying in Jesus' name signifies asking for things that are in accordance with His will so that their fulfillment brings glory and honor to the name of God!

Additionally, we have to ask God for it, and we have to do so with the right motives (James 4:2-3). God will prosper us as we place our trust in Him and desire to do His will. It is His working in us and through us that ensures our success, but we have to ask. If we lean upon God only as a last resort, we will miss the answer to many unspoken needs.

God's Plans, Not Ours

Scripture unequivocally states that before you were ever conceived, God had a plan for your life. Among other things, this includes good works that will bring forth fruit for His kingdom. And God created *you* to do them! We are not saved *by* good works; rather, we are saved in order *to do* good works. Good works are the evidence of salvation, not the reason behind it. Read Jeremiah 29:11, Psalm 139:16, and Ephesians 2:8-10.

In these verses, we see that we were created with divine purpose to bring God glory and honor, to do good works, and to be godly in character. God didn't create us to do just any good works; He created us to do specific good works. In other words, before you ever existed, God prepared a specific set of good deeds for you to accomplish while on this earth. This means that we should ask God what He wants us to accomplish for Him rather than blundering off on our own.

For many years I asked God to walk with me and bless my efforts. At the time I thought I was praying a very noble prayer, but do you see how self-centered it is? I asked God to join me as I decided what I would do for God through my efforts, and I expected God to bless me in return.

That was a completely backwards prayer. No wonder I was often left confused and disappointed when my prayers went unanswered. Even though I ended my prayers "in Jesus' name," it had no meaning. I was not praying in God's will because I was motivated by a desire to remain in charge while asking God along merely as my helper.

We should never engage in any service for the Lord without first waiting on Him for direction. He is the Lord, and we are only His servants, seeking to do His sovereign will. God wants us to walk with Him, and He wants us to observe what He is doing. If God has saved us by His grace, then He has saved us for a life of good works—and He wants to reveal them to us!

Discovering Your Purpose

Discovering your purpose is a topic that goes beyond the scope of this book, but I would like to briefly mention a number of things for you to consider. During our time together we have looked extensively at several of these points.

- Believe and recognize that you have a purpose.

- Believe that God is in control. No one but you can thwart your destiny. Stop blaming others for your negative circumstances.

- If you want to know God's will, get to know God. He wants an intimate relationship with you. Start by reading His Word and asking Him to draw you closer to Him.

- Obey His will as revealed in the Bible. He will not give you additional insight if you won't be obedient to what He has already made clear.

- Don't dictate to God what your ministry should be. Stop asking God to "bless me in my endeavors" and start asking Him to reveal what He wants you to do for His glory.

- Discover your gifts. God gives you gifts, abilities, and talents, and He wants you to use them in your sphere of influence. They are not that hard to discover, for no matter where you are or what your circumstances are, your gifts will surface. They will be things you like to do, and engaging in them will excite and energize you. Volunteer for various ministries. You will quickly discover what drains you and what turns you on. Ask those who know you for feedback.

- Discover your direction and go forth. As your gifts become discernable, they will point you in a general direction. God determines the path we should follow, but we, by our faithfulness and perseverance, decide how far along that road we will travel. As you responsibly and faithfully walk in that direction, God will give you additional insight, and you will eventually fulfill your purpose.

- Don't expect to know the specifics up front. A vision of your whole life's plan will not flash before your eyes. God's wisdom and knowledge are like a flashlight on a moonless night (Psalm 119:105). Have you ever taken a walk along a rugged path in the dark? Not only do you depend heavily on your flashlight for safety, but you also proceed very slowly because you are unable to see more than a few steps ahead of you. Like the flashlight, God wants us to form a daily dependence upon Him. If you knew your whole life's plan, you would either be terrified of the insurmountable challenges ahead, or you would run off on your own and leave God in the dust. For that reason He gives us just enough information to accomplish the immediate task that He has for us—and this, also, in increments.

You Have a Choice

As you follow God's lead you will experience true biblical prosperity. God does not want us to be lacking in anything. He wants to shower us with "great and precious promises" and to provide us with "everything we need for life and godliness" (2 Peter 1:3-4).

Don't be surprised, however, when you experience setbacks and apparent failures. Remember Joseph? Through it all God expects us to forge ahead on the path He has chosen for us. The only way we are going to have any meaningful impact on this world is for others around us to see that our faith in Christ is genuine and that it is effective and practical through the ups and downs of our daily lives.

God has an awesome plan for each of us, but He will not force it upon anyone. We do not have to cooperate with Him. We can live our entire lives here on earth barren, unfruitful, and unfulfilled. But know this: God is sovereign, and the good works that He planned before creation itself will be accomplished, if need be by someone else. Yet we have a wonderful opportunity to decide whether or not we are going to participate.

Many of God's promises are unconditional, but blessing, fruitfulness, and victory over our trials are not. You must turn your fears, anxieties, doubts, apathy, and selfishness over to Him. In return He will give you unfathomable blessings and the deep fulfillment that has always eluded the unspoken longings of the human heart.

The only thing related to our earthy existence that will reverberate throughout all eternity are the good things that we allow God to work in us, thereby fulfilling that which He called us to do. The Bible tells us (1 Corinthians 3:12-15) that Christ is the only foundation upon which we can build our lives. If any man builds upon Christ, he will be saved. His work, however, will not survive if he uses inferior materials—such as good things done apart from Christ and with wrong motives. The Day of Judgment will reveal the quality of each person's work. God will determine whether or not the laborer has been faithful to Jesus' instructions. Good work (gold, silver, costly stones) will be rewarded, but unfaithful work (wood, hay, straw) will be burned up.

We are called to many purposes in this life: to know God and to believe Him, to serve as His witness, to grow in Christ-like character, to endure hardships and trials, to love and encourage one another, and to accomplish good works. A flourishing faith is the driving force that keeps us pressing on in obedience.

Prayer Time

Father,

I thank You for Your abundant grace and willingness to aid me in every circumstance of life, be it hardship or ease. I trust in Your promise to bless me in the things that You have called me to accomplish. Help me to accept Your sovereign right to rule over me. Give me a heart that longs to obey You, a heart that seeks hard after You. I confidently pray these things by the authority granted me in Jesus Christ, Your Beloved Son. Amen!

Cultivating Your Garden of Faith

Get It Straight:

1. Ephesians 1:3 tells us that we are blessed with "every spiritual blessing in Christ." Read the rest of Ephesians 1, Romans 8, Psalm 103, and Galatians 5:22. What spiritual blessings do you find there? Can you think of other spiritual blessings? Where in the Bible are they mentioned?

2. How does true godly obedience differ from legalism?

3. What are all the implications when we pray in Jesus' name?

4. How do good works and salvation tie together? Are James and Paul at odds regarding the issue of faith? (Romans 5:1-2, Ephesians 2:4-10, James 2:14-25) Explain.

Head to Heart:

1. Read the Ten Commandments (Exodus 20:1-17). For each commandment think about why obeying it is actually for your welfare.

2. In our culture today pastors are sometimes forbidden to pray "in Jesus' name" when invited to pray at public gatherings. Do you think a Christian should bow to this request/demand? (Explain.) Do you think something important is being stripped from a prayer when this phrase is deliberately omitted? (Explain.)

3. What gifts and abilities has God given you? If you don't know, how can you find out? Ask others for some feedback. Has what they said surprised you?

You and God:

1. Which aspect(s) of worldly success do you desire the most (money, possessions, fame, beauty, status, power, other)? Why?

2. On a scale of 1 to 10 how worldly successful do you consider yourself to be? On a scale of 1 to 10 how rich are you toward God?

3. How has the desire for success affected you? How has it affected your relationship with God and others?

4. 1 Timothy 6:6 says, "Godliness with contentment is great gain." Take a sheet of paper and divide it up into the following categories:

- relationships
  (list at least four sub-categories: God; family; friends; others)
- health-physical/emotional
- financial
- work
- leisure
- geographical
- church
- pets/animals
- abilities/skills
- miscellaneous

Under each category list things you are thankful for. If a certain category seems particularly dismal to you, make a special effort to think of at least a few blessings. Use this list as a prayer of thanksgiving to God. SAVE THIS LIST! We will add to it in the final chapter of this book.

5. How convinced are you that God has specific plans for you to bear fruit for His kingdom? (Use the 1–10 scale.) In what ways have you been a blessing to others?

Scripture Memory

I have two verses for you to memorize this time. I know that this will be twice the effort, but if you keep them in your heart, they will be a great encouragement to you.

But the man who looks intently into the perfect law that gives freedom, and continues to do this, not forgetting what he has heard, but doing it—he will be blessed in what he does. (James 1:25)

If you remain in me and my words remain in you, ask whatever you wish, and it will be given you. This is to my Father's glory, that you bear much fruit, showing yourselves to be my disciples. (John 15:7-8)

Personal Thoughts:

_____

_____

_____

_____

_____

Trusting God When Life Hurts:
(I Can't Believe I Did That!)

Who can discern his errors?
Forgive my hidden faults.
Keep your servant also from willful sins;
may they not rule over me.
Then will I be blameless,
innocent of great transgression.
(Psalm 19:12-13)

My father was a devoted family man who held fast to the "spare the rod, spoil the child" philosophy. He was also very handy with wood. One of his more notorious projects was a paddle made out of pine. When one of us would smart off or otherwise misbehave, he would put it to use on our posteriors. Although my oldest brother, Ron, would panic the moment punishment seemed inevitable, I was by far more dramatic. By the time my father returned with the paddle, I was crying so hysterically I usually got off easy. My other brother Paul, however, was both stubborn and stoic; he never uttered a sound during his spankings. As a result he always received the most swats. I suppose my father figured Paul wasn't learning his lesson.

One day while snooping through the hall linen closet I came across The Dreaded Thing. Temptation got the better of me, and I hid it at the back of the closet beneath some rags that hadn't been used in years. My devious plan succeeded; my brothers and I were spared several spankings because my father couldn't find the paddle.

I was never successful at hiding from my Heavenly Father. Unlike my earthly father, God cannot be tricked or outsmarted.

Discipline hurts, and it's difficult to accept that sin or poor choices caused the pain in our lives, especially if we knew our motives were harmless. As Christians, we may get caught up in unintentional sin. In fact, sometimes our motives are quite pure; we meant to help a hurting friend, but out of ignorance we exercised poor judgment and let our friend pull us into the pit.

My friend Anne got caught in a trap like this. Her brother Ed and his wife, Meg, were going through an ugly divorce. Anne was very close to both of them. She met Meg for lunch one day in order to give her comfort. In the course of the conversation, Meg began ranting about how Ed had hurt and used her. Anne felt uncomfortable with the conversation, but instead of telling Meg she didn't feel right about getting involved in a discussion involving her brother, she ignored her feelings and continued to listen and give sympathy to Meg. A few weeks later, Meg lost control of her emotions, telling Ed that his own sister sided with her. The next day Anne got an earful from Ed, who told her that he did not want her to see Meg any more. While Meg was wrong for pitting Anne against her own brother, Anne exercised poor judgment for allowing herself to be dragged into the gossip. As a result Anne was forced to make a painful choice between Meg and her brother.

Perhaps we didn't realize that a certain behavior or attitude was sinful and took no action to curb it until it became deeply entrenched in our life, or maybe a seemingly harmless distraction turned into an obsession, stronghold, or idol.

I got caught up in the excitement of building a vacation home in the woods near Flagstaff, Arizona. As the time grew closer to its completion, I spent my spare time shopping for bed-and-bath items, kitchen supplies, and knick-knacks. I have always loved the woods, so I enjoyed daydreaming about what it would be like to spend weekends there with my husband and the dogs. Two months later I woke up depressed, wondering where my joy of the Lord had gone. God's presence seemed absent from my life. Without realizing it that vacation home had become a higher priority in my life than God. Instead of reading His Word, I went shopping; rather than spending time in prayer, I visualized what my finished home would look like; instead of worshiping Him, I spent Sunday mornings refinishing an old dresser. By my actions, I had inadvertently told God that having a house in the woods was more fulfilling to me than He was. Those were distressing days for me, and returning God to His rightful place in my life was a painful process.

There is nothing inherently evil about having a vacation home or enjoying the earthly blessings that God gives us, but putting those things above God clearly violates His First and Second Commandments: "You shall have no other gods before me. You shall not make for yourself an idol" (Exodus 20:3-4). Our Lord had good reason for ordering His commandments as He did, for nothing will kill your faith and destroy your fellowship with Him faster than a false god.

As a child I thought those commandments didn't apply anymore. I thought idols were stone images that ancient people bowed to. I didn't realize that gods and idols come in many shapes and sizes: a person or a relationship; money and possessions; substances such as food, cigarettes, drugs, alcohol; a desire for physical beauty; a need for approval or good reputation; a hunger for power, status, or sexual encounters.

Some idols are so firmly entrenched in our lives that only God can remove them. Addictive sin may result when we turn to things or other people rather than to God in an attempt to cope with pain and emptiness in our lives. Our actions often begin in ignorance but soon progress to a lifestyle of sin from which its victims cannot escape. The thing that used to satisfy no longer does, and when caught in this trap we indulge ourselves more frequently and with greater intensity. Eventually no matter how much we partake, we are not satisfied (Ephesians 4:17-19). The consequences are devastating, but we no longer care, for nothing becomes more important than "the fix." Healing can occur only after we recognize the existence of idols in our lives, admit that we cannot be satisfied, and turn back to God.

Sometimes our sin is purely reactive. A sudden, unexpected situation causes our emotions to flare, and we say or do something we regret later. While our ungodly reaction was neither planned nor expected, the sinful attitude was there all along, lurking beneath the surface; the unanticipated circumstance simply drew it out. An unkind putdown or a false accusation may result in an uncontrolled outburst of profanity, anger, or pride.

It may be that our sin has taken on more of a premeditated tone, such as seeking revenge on someone who has hurt us, planning an affair, or devising a clever lie to get what we want. Have you ever deliberately sinned, knowing that God will forgive you for it the next day? Consider your answer carefully; I'm not just talking about the "big" sins. I think about the times I went to an all-you-can-eat buffet wearing stretch pants and a baggy top. As I was feeling the first wave of temptation, even before I put any food into my mouth, I thought to myself, "I feel bad that I'm going to gorge myself, but I can't help it; the food looks so good! Oh well, I will get right with God about this tomorrow morning when I start my new diet." Gluttony is premeditated sin!

The real issue behind deliberate disobedience is the fact that we neither believe God nor trust Him; we care far more about what we want than what God wants. We may think He is holding out on us, that His laws are not for our benefit. Or we may think we can disobey God and get away with it. Please be very careful about adopting such a casual attitude toward sin. We are told to guard our heart because it is the wellspring of life (Proverbs 4:23). Our motives are very important to God. Playing the sin-oops!-confess game with Him is extremely dangerous, because the stakes are high and you will lose—*guaranteed!* God will not allow us to mock Him and get away with it unscathed (Galatians 6:7-8).

Of course, God will forgive us when we finally come to Him in true repentance. The longer we try to play games with God, the deeper we will get into sin, and the harder it will be for us to repent. God hates sin not only because it is contrary to His nature, but because it greatly harms us. If we choose to harden our heart for too long of a period, we may reach a point where we lose the desire to get right with Him.

Because God eagerly desires for us to triumph over our temptations, He always gives us warning signs along with a means of escape (1 Corinthians 10:12-13).

If the Holy Spirit lives in you, you have a built in alarm system warning you of impending sin. We can choose to turn it off, thinking that the uncomfortable feeling within is nothing more than overactive worry, or we can deliberately switch it off knowing full well that we are quenching the Holy Spirit. Discretion is the freedom to make wise decisions. Compulsive behavior hides our choices from us. God in His mercy returns our freedom of choice, but He always leaves the final decision to us (Proverbs 2:6-11).

> *"Everything is permissible for me—but not everything is beneficial. Everything is permissible for me—but I will not be mastered by anything." (1 Corinthians 6:12)*

No Place for Self-Condemnation

You are God's beloved child; never be afraid to turn to Him after you have sinned or acted unwisely! God is compassionate and full of mercy. He longs to bestow His grace and abundant blessing upon you. See for yourself in Psalm 103:2-5, 10-12.

The fact that we act foolishly does not diminish His love for us. His love is unconditional and has nothing to do with our performance; it's all about who He is (1 John 4:16). Yes, He does rebuke us, but His motive is to draw us back to Him for restoration. We need to trust Him to restore and heal us when our disobedience has resulted in painful consequences.

Repentance

Those whom I love I rebuke and discipline. So be earnest, and repent. (Revelation 3:19)

The first thing God asks of us after we have sinned is to repent. The Greek word for *repent* is *metanoeo*. It means to rethink or to change one's mind. In biblical terms this means changing the way we think about our sins—that is, seeing our sins as God sees them. Only then will we stop making excuses and get serious about identifying and eliminating the deceptions and rationalizations that lead us into the sinful behavior. If we continue to see our sins as pleasurable, amusing, or attractive rather than repulsive and evil, we are not seeing them from God's point of view and have not repented. Do you ever laugh at dirty jokes? Are you amused when an intoxicated person does silly things at a party? If so you are not seeing sin as God sees it, and you are not repentant over the impurity and overindulgent desires that lurk in your own heart.

Genuine repentance always leads to a heartfelt confession of sin. The Greek word for *confession* is *homologeo*. It means to say the same thing that another says. Confession is the act of saying the same thing about our sin that God says. Repentance and confession are intimately linked, for we cannot say what God says about our sin until we first change our minds about our sin, seeing it as God sees it.

If we claim to be without sin, we deceive ourselves and the truth is not in us. If we confess our sins, he is faithful and just and will forgive us our sins and purify us from all unrighteousness. (1 John 1:8-9)

When you became a Christian you were forgiven and cleansed of all your sins—past, present, and *future!* (1 Peter 3:18). Your relationship with God is secure because of what Christ did on the cross. Even though all of your sins have already been forgiven, you still need to deal with them daily because your fellowship with God is interrupted when you choose to sin. As a Christian your fellowship with God is restored as soon as you:

- repent of your sins
- confess them
- thank Him for having *already forgiven* your transgressions
- turn away from sin and back to God

God also wants us to make things right with others we may have offended. When we have done wrong we must be willing to take responsibility for our mistakes. We cannot be right with God if we do not seek reconciliation with the ones affected by our sin (Matthew 5:23-24).

If we persist in making excuses for our behavior or blaming others, we will continue to struggle with selfishness, dishonesty, gossip, anger, bitterness, jealousy, and lust along with a multitude of other relational problems. We will never get a grip on the fear, worry, depression, or self-hatred that occasionally paralyzes us. God wants us to openly confess our sin instead of trying to cover it up. Confession will be easier for us to do once we realize that we have been fully forgiven by God. We no longer have to bear the awful load of self-condemnation.

Godly Sorrow vs. Worldly Sorrow

Repentance begins with sorrow, but not all sorrow leads to repentance. There is a vast difference between Godly sorrow and worldly sorrow; one leads to life, the other to death.

yet now I am happy, not because you were made sorry, but because your sorrow led you to repentance. For you became sorrowful as God intended and so were not harmed in any way by us. Godly sorrow brings repentance that leads to salvation and leaves no regret, but worldly sorrow brings death. (2 Corinthians 7:9-10)

Both types of sorrow produce anguish within the soul. Let's take a closer look at the differences between genuine sorrow and worldly sorrow.

Godly Sorrow	Worldly Sorrow
Genuine sorrow over sin	Shallow, temporary remorse over undesired consequences
Seeks the truth about sin	Surrounds itself with deception
Leads to repentance	Filled with empty promises
Orchestrated by God through Holy Spirit's conviction [John 16:8]	Devised by Satan
Results in change	Is unable to break the cycle of sin, confess, try again
God-Centered: The sorrow comes from knowing that God's will was despised.	Self-Centered: the sorrow comes from the painful circumstances we find ourselves in
Focuses on the wrong thinking that led to the sin	Focuses on the end result or the consequences of the sin.
Generates true forgiveness with no regret	Generates self-condemnation and useless regret
Results in a desire to turn toward God to seek forgiveness	Results in shame and a strong desire to hide or run away from God.
Results in spiritual life—a true confession of sin, an acknowledgment that Christ died on the cross for our sins, an invitation for Christ to be Lord and Savior of our lives	Results in a lifetime of half-hearted attempts to change that eventually leads to spiritual death.
Says things like: "Thank You for loving me in spite of my sin; thank You for forgiving me and making me clean; I am grateful that You will never leave me nor abandon me; thank You for your loving discipline; I know that You will lead me through this and I will be more Christ-like in the end."	Says things like: "Sorry I got caught; sorry I got that disease; sorry I lost my reputation and self-respect; sorry I can no longer fit into my clothes; sorry that my marriage failed; sorry I'm depressed and hurting; why don't I learn; why did I do such a stupid thing; why do I keep hurting the ones I love?

Do you see why worldly sorrow cannot lead to repentance and confession of sin? In our misery we focus on ourselves and automatically shut God out. We cannot look beyond ourselves in order to determine how God views our sin. We are unable to see past our sickness in order to discover God's cure for our hopeless state. We stay stuck in *our* misery, *our* guilt, *our* shame, *our* remorse, *our* stinking-thinking until we collapse into a wretched state of despair.

True repentance involves deep sorrow, but the grief and shame we feel is over our sin as we begin to realize our own impurity before a Holy God. The prophet Isaiah experienced this and reacted in great distress.

Woe to me!" I cried. "I am ruined! For I am a man of unclean lips, and I live among a people of unclean lips, and my eyes have seen the King, the LORD Almighty. (Isaiah 6:5)

God had to send His only Son into the world to atone for our sins. Jesus—the One who created all things, the Lord and Giver of life, the Lover of our souls, the Alpha and the Omega, the great I AM, the King of Kings and Lord of Lords—was mocked, beaten, and spat upon. His beard was ripped from His face. He was flogged with hideous whips that tore His flesh to ribbons; a crown of thorns was cruelly thrust upon His head. Most men would not have survived this torture, but He did, and still that was not enough. He was humiliated and made to carry His own cross while the crowd jeered. Finally, He was nailed to a rough wooden cross and crucified.

God allowed His Son to die in such anguish so that you and I would be brought back into fellowship with Him. Only when we see our sin for what it is, the reason for Christ's suffering, will we be able to experience the sorrow of a repentant heart.

Or do you show contempt for the riches of his kindness, tolerance and patience, not realizing that God's kindness leads you toward repentance? (Romans 2:4)

Being perfect before God is not a matter of never failing; it is a question of what we do about it when we do fall. God loves us, and the pain He allows us to suffer for our sin is meant to bring us to Him. If we are doing everything we can to hide from God, then we are falling prey to The Lie. Condemnation is not from God; it is from Satan. The Holy Spirit will convict us when necessary, but He will never condemn us.

Therefore, there is now no condemnation for those who are in Christ Jesus. (Romans 8:1)

The Bible informs us that Satan is the accuser of the brethren (Revelation 12:10) and the father of lies (John 8:44). Satan knows he can't have us, so he does the next "best" thing; he tries to mess up our thinking through deception. His diabolical plot is to:

• darken and confuse our mind, hide our choices from us.

• render us helpless and ineffective against his dark kingdom by filling us with fear.

• nullify our testimony so that others will look at our life and see nothing desirable about it.

• demolish significant human relationships.

• damage our intimacy with God, entice us to sin, and then make us feel guilty for falling so that we will run away from God.

• destroy all sense of godly significance through guilt, shame, and self-condemnation.

• lead us away from the magnificent plans and mission God has for us.

Satan's powerful snare is well-camouflaged; once caught we will stay in it until we move from worldly sorrow to godly sorrow. We will remain a captive to sin until we dump the lies that are floating around in our head.

The only way to counteract lies is with The Truth. We will talk more about defusing lies in the final chapter of this book, but for now, realize that God is most eager to set us free from all deception.

God gave each of us a free will. All too often we use it to get ourselves into trouble by making sinful or foolish choices. However, after we have had a change of heart, God expects us to use our will to formulate a plan of action for both restoration and victory over every area of our life. We can resolve to "go and sin no more." Repentance is a gift from God (2 Timothy 2:25), and He will lead us to knowledge and truth as we study His Word and lean upon Him for our guidance and understanding (Proverbs 3:5-6).

As long as you have a pulse, it is not too late. No matter how guilty you feel for making things worse, God still has a wonderful plan for your life; He still wants to use you to make a difference in this troubled world. It happened for Chuck Colson, and it can happen for you.

From 1969 to 1973 Chuck Colson acted as Special Counsel for President Richard Nixon. In summing up his role Colson wrote,

> If I was valuable to the President, … it was because I was willing at times to blink at certain ethical standards, to be ruthless in getting things done. It was earning me status and power. … Getting the job done for the President whatever the cost—earned me also the dubious title of Nixon's 'hatchet man.'[1]

In his determination to get Nixon reelected, Colson had even once joked that "I would walk over my grandmother if necessary."[2]

In the early 1970s Colson became involved in the Watergate and Daniel Ellsberg scandals. As his world came crashing down around him, he visited his old friend, Tom Phillips, who gave him a copy of C. S. Lewis' book *Mere Christianity.* Lewis' words affected him greatly. Colson wrote, "The truth, I saw in an instant, was that I'd wanted the position in the White House more than I'd wanted money. … I would eagerly have given up everything I'd ever earned to prove myself at the mountaintop of government. It was pride—Lewis's 'great sin'—that had propelled me through life."[3] That very evening in August 1973, Chuck Colson turned his shattered life over to Christ.

Although he believed himself to be innocent in the Watergate cover-up, he wanted to completely clear his conscience. Following prayer and discussion with his fellowship group, Colson pleaded guilty to a different charge—one for which he did consider himself culpable: smearing Ellsberg while he was under indictment for releasing the so-called Pentagon Papers to the press.

Colson was given a one- to three-year sentence but was released after seven months due to a family hardship. During his time in prison, Colson became aware of the injustices often done to prisoners and the inadequacy of prisoner rehabilitation. As Colson witnessed God working in the lives of some of his fellow inmates, he became increasingly convinced that God had called him to prison ministry; thus, after being released, Colson founded Prison Fellowship. His life touches thousands of men and women in prison every year, and through Prison Fellowship he and others have diligently worked to promote prisoner rehabilitation and reform. Chuck Colson became one of the greatest Christian leaders in our world today and, as an author and speaker, has had a profound impact on our world for Christ.

As with all sin and pain, God will use the negative consequences to bless you—*if* you let Him. Do you remember the verse from 2 Corinthians 7:10 that we looked at earlier in this chapter? "Godly sorrow brings repentance that leads to salvation and *leaves no regret.*" The genuine sorrow you experienced was produced by the Holy Spirit in order to bring about your repentance. Once this is accomplished, it leaves no regret, only a joy of the Lord. You can come away from your heartbreaks with greater wisdom and a wonderful, flourishing faith. Through restoration you are blessed by Him to be a partaker of God's grace, and you can share that with a hurting world. You can use what you learned to help others still trapped in sin.

Prayer Time

Oh Gracious Father,
Thank You for your loving discipline. I know it was given for my benefit. I know You will lead me safely, and my regret will be transformed into joy. Thank You for sending Your Son to die for my sins so that I could be forgiven and made whole again. Thank You cleansing me from every transgression—past, present, and future and for restoring my fellowship with You. Amen.

Cultivating Your Garden of Faith

Get It Straight:

1. Read the story of the prodigal son (Luke 15:11-32). In verse 17, what does the text tell us about his thinking? What things did the prodigal son do and say that indicate he was repentant? What was his father's response? What does this teach us about God's willingness to forgive us?

2. Read the story of Zacchaeus (Luke 19:1-9). What things did Zacchaeus do and say that demonstrate he was repentant? What was Jesus' response?

3. Read Psalm 32. What did David experience before he confessed his sin? How did he feel after he acknowledged his sin? Can you relate to this?

Head to Heart:

1. In addition to the ones listed in this chapter, what false gods/idols/addictions can you think of that people in today's culture tend to get caught up in?

2. Why is premeditated sin so serious?

3. Why do we tend to hide from God when we do something wrong? What steps can we take to get back into fellowship with Him?

You and God:

1. Can you think of a time when you truly repented? If so, how do you know it was godly sorrow and not worldly sorrow? What was the result?

2. An idol is anything we try to replace God with. What idols have a hold on you? What dissatisfactions in life cause you to turn to your idol(s)?

3. Are there sins you struggle with again and again? If so, what are they?

4. What is making it hard for you to repent from these things?

Scripture Memory

If we confess our sins, he is faithful and just and will forgive us our sins and purify us from all unrighteousness. (1 John 1:9)

Personal Thoughts:

_____

_____

_____

_____

_____

Chapter 10

Taking Every Thought Captive:
Battling Discouraging Thoughts

> We demolish arguments and every pretension that sets
> itself up against the knowledge of God, and we take
> captive every thought to make it obedient to Christ.
> (2 Corinthians 10:5)

The Diamond Machine

There once was an unethical salesman named Fred who traveled the country. One day Fred came upon a naive but very greedy man named Nick, who spent all his time dreaming about acquiring diamonds. After unsuccessfully trying to sell Nick some tools, Fred pulled out a strange-looking contraption, which he called a diamond machine. Fred assured Nick that this machine would faithfully produce diamonds from sand as long as he followed a few simple instructions. He then produced a lifetime, money-back guarantee in writing. Nick's eyes lit up as Fred proceeded to explain the operating instructions: "First press the green 'on' button located on top of the machine. Place a bucket underneath the chute labeled 'diamond drop' and put five scoops of sand in the funnel. Next push the yellow 'start' button. After about five minutes, the diamonds will automatically drop into the bucket." Gleefully imagining the fortune he would make selling the diamonds, Nick quickly purchased the device for $100. As he started to leave, Fred called after him: "Stop! I almost forgot to tell you the most important instruction of all. Under no circumstance during any part of the diamond-making process are you to think about the color purple. If you do, the machine will fail to produce diamonds." Nick nodded his head as he walked away to find some sand. He thought to himself, "Since that's the most important instruction, I'd better put a note on the machine reminding me never to think about purple."

Everyday, for the rest of his life, Nick faithfully operated the diamond machine in an attempt to produce a wealth of diamonds; unfortunately, the color purple always popped into his mind during the critical steps. Sadly, not one diamond ever came out of the machine, and Nick eventually died disappointed and penniless.

The Peaceful, Steadfast Mind

Has the enemy placed unwanted thoughts in your mind that you can't seem to get rid of no matter how hard you try?

This final chapter has to do with our thought life. It's an important topic for us to consider, because unrestrained, unhealthy thoughts will kill our faith at the "speed of thought." Our faith can and will work for us in down-to-earth, practical ways only as we allow Christ to become Lord of our minds.

I would like to give some practical ways to deal with detrimental thinking, but first let's look at a few reassuring promises from the Bible.

You will keep in perfect peace him whose mind is steadfast, because he trusts in you. Trust in the LORD forever, for the LORD, the LORD, is the Rock eternal. (Isaiah 26:3-4)

These verses assure us that we can rely upon the Lord because He is a solid, stable foundation that will never crumble. As we get to know God in this manner we will increasingly depend upon Him for all our needs. This deep and abiding trust leads to a steadfast mind—or, as The King James Version puts it, a person "whose mind is stayed on thee." God faithfully promises His perfect peace to the person with a steadfast mind.

This is an amazing promise, so let's nail down what the Bible means by a steadfast mind. The Hebrew word *yetser* appears in most translations as *mind*. It means purpose, frame, pattern, imagination. As applied to our minds, it is the frame of reference or point of view from which we consistently interpret things around us; it is our mind-set.

The English word *steadfast* or *stayed* represents the Hebrew verb *camak*. It means to lay, rest; to lean against, rest upon or rely on; to support or sustain.

A steadfast mind is a faith-filled mind that chooses to see all life events through the *framework* of God and His Word. It is a trusting mind that decides to *rest or rely upon* God's promises. It is a stable mind that *consistently lays* its harmful desires and anxious thoughts and concerns in God's capable hands. This is possible because the steadfast mind is focused on God, the eternal Rock.

The benefit of a steadfast mind is perfect peace. Most of us have heard the Hebrew word *shalom*, but it encompasses much more than our narrow concept of peace. In addition to external peace and friendship, it means completeness, soundness, health, safety, security, tranquility, and welfare in body, soul, and spirit. It is a serene and blessed absence of troubled, disturbing thoughts. This is the same peace that Jesus spoke about when He said, "Peace I leave with you; my peace I give you. I do not give to you as the world gives. Do not let your hearts be troubled and do not be afraid" (John 14:27).

The world can't give this kind of peace, and the world can't take it away. On this troubled, violent planet, who doesn't long for this kind of deep, abiding peace!

But these verses convey a still more powerful concept, which is found in the word *keep*. This Hebrew verb, *natsar*, means to watch over; to preserve, to guard from dangers.

There is more to peace than *staying* or *resting* one's mind on positive thoughts and emotions. I don't doubt people who tell me they experience inner peace when they meditate on positive things such as human kindness. I can relate. As an animal-lover, I experience the same thing whenever I see puppies romping together. But there is more to "inner peace" than wagging tails or a heart-warming story of human triumph. As pleasant as these things are for us, this type of inner peace is temporary and will shatter the moment we hear bad news.

In contrast, only God is able to supernaturally guard our minds as we fix our thoughts on Him—*actively working* to preserve our right thinking while carefully shielding it from the fiery darts of the enemy! And who better qualified for the job than our loving, sovereign Creator who knows and understands our every thought (Psalm 139:1-4, 23)?

This was vividly demonstrated to me more than nineteen years ago when my beloved mother died one week after my birthday. Apart from God, no one understood me better or loved me more than my mother, and how I loved her! Throughout my life she was my confidante and dearest friend. I couldn't imagine life without her, so understandably some of my most fearful thoughts were about losing her.

While mourning my mother's passing, the Lord's manifest presence never left me. The day after her memorial service, I remember standing alone in the kitchen, picturing my mother in the loving arms of Jesus. As I continued to ponder this, an incomprehensible sense of joy and peace washed over me. I could neither express it nor explain it, but I was immensely grateful to God for guarding my thoughts during those painful days.

Of course there are times when I miss my mother deeply. Even as I write this, the longing to see her again fills my eyes with tears. But I never think about my mother without inviting the One who holds the keys to life and eternity into the center of my thoughts; He never fails to keep my soul at peace.

Good feelings come and go, and pleasant experiences are all too often replaced with painful ones, but our covenant-keeping God promises to guard and preserve the peace of those whose mind is stayed on Him, as you'll read in Philippians 4:4-7.

We can see in these passages the concept of a steadfast mind as Paul encourages his readers to frame the context of their lives with an attitude of joy, gentleness, prayerfulness, and thanksgiving.

Paul assures us that we can trust the Lord to help us because we know that He is always near to us as our mind is stayed upon Him. We are to reveal our inner peace by being outwardly patient, gentle, and gracious to others. We are also urged to lay down our anxious thoughts by turning them over to God in prayer and petition with thanksgiving.

As we have discussed at length, this kind of rejoicing is born only of faith that trusts in God and His promises. We are able to rejoice in everything when we look past our present circumstances to the good that we know will come out of our painful circumstances if we do not lose faith and hope.

Prayer and petition along with gratitude for what God can do is an indispensible part of overcoming destructive thoughts. We will address these concepts a little later in this chapter.

Spiritual Warfare

It is vitally important to know who or what wars against our mind and discover how we can work with God in order to be victorious over our thought life. The following verses give us much insight:

For though we live in the world, we do not wage war as the world does. The weapons we fight with are not the weapons of the world. On the contrary, they have divine power to demolish strongholds. We demolish arguments and every pretension that sets itself up against the knowledge of God, and we take captive every thought to make it obedient to Christ. (2 Corinthians 10:3-5)

First, notice that God provides us with weapons that are not of this world. Many nations have developed fearful weapons known as weapons of mass destruction (WMD). The weapons referred to in these verses are much more powerful! They are <u>W</u>eapons of <u>D</u>ivine <u>P</u>ower (WDP) and are used to demolish highly pervasive and destructive thoughts.

The Greek noun *ochuroma* refers to a stronghold, fortress, or castle. Used metaphorically here, strongholds are wrong thoughts and perceptions that contradict the knowledge and nature of God. They are places of refuge that we have built over the years for security and reassurance. Strongholds are anything we rely on apart from God. Unfortunately, during the construction process we fail to realize that we are erecting our own prisons!

Can you relate to any of these strongholds?

- **Idols:** a co-dependent relationship; a fixation upon a celebrity, materialism, an obsession to be beautiful, an unhealthy drive for power, a need for approval

- **Addictions and compulsive behaviors:** drugs, alcohol, gambling, overeating, shopping, watching TV, computer games or Internet, profanity, pornography

- **Obsessive thoughts:** fear, worry, depression, false guilt, food, sexual fantasies

- **Wrong attitudes or beliefs:** feelings of worthlessness, self-pity, racial bigotry, envy, hatred, negativism, bitterness, self-righteousness, self-sufficiency

The Greek word for *arguments* is *logismos*. This refers to a reasoning, consideration, or reflection. In this context, these are the rationalizations and excuses we use in order to keep our strongholds intact. They strengthen and justify our position and sooth our conscience so that we do not feel it necessary to surrender our strongholds to the authority of Christ!

Hupsoma is Greek for *pretension*. It refers to an elevated structure such as a barrier or rampart. In ancient times strongholds were built on elevated places to make them impenetrable. Used metaphorically, a pretension is something or someone that we have placed on a pedestal or in a position of honor. Similarly, every stronghold we embrace is linked to something that wrongly holds a higher position in our lives than God. Often it is something about which we are prideful.

These arguments and pretensions set themselves up against the knowledge of God. Strongholds and the rationalizations that defend them are always based on lies. The truth is an essential Weapon of Divine Power for demolishing strongholds along with the proud and lofty rationalizations we cling to. It is the only way we can be free (John 8:32). In a postmodern culture that denies the concept of absolute truth in the spiritual and moral spheres, this is a weapon sorely needed by the church.

The war terms Paul uses produce very powerful images. I imagine our thoughts as soldiers out of uniform. Each one is a potential enemy spy pretending to be "friendly," but in reality it is a deadly foe ready to strike at an opportune time. How do we determine which side of the battle our thoughts are on? We take them all captive and interrogate each one according to the truth of God. Those thoughts that prove to be enemies to the knowledge of God are made subject to Christ. Easier said than done, isn't it! Fortunately, the apostle Paul helps us with the interrogation process:

*Finally, brothers, whatever is true, whatever is noble, whatever
is right, whatever is pure, whatever is lovely, whatever is
admirable—if anything is excellent or praiseworthy—think
about such things. (Philippians 4:8)*

- True—as measured by God and His Word.

- Noble—honorable or worthy of respect.

- Right—or righteous as defined by God and His character.

- Pure—whatever is unblemished by evil.

- Lovely—lovable or enjoyable. While more of a worldly term
  that has nothing to do with morality, the context in which
  this word appears strongly indicates that we should filter the
  "enjoyable" things of this world through God's Word.

- Admirable—this represents the kind of conduct that is
  worth considering because it is well-spoken of by people in
  general; this also is to be filtered through the Bible.

- Excellent—Christian virtue or moral excellence.

- Praiseworthy—conduct that is in keeping with God's own
  righteousness.

The enemy has held us prisoner through destructive wrong
thinking. Only by surrendering our thoughts to Christ and fixing
our mind completely on Him will we free ourselves from unhealthy,
negative thoughts. Successfully taking our thoughts captive does
not mean we will never think those thoughts again. It simply means
that we are to examine them in light of who we are in Christ. If our
thoughts don't line up with Christ and His Words, we are to regard
them as enemy spies. Next, Paul tells us *who* the enemy is in Ephesians
6:10-12. Please look these passages up in your Bible.

Satan is devious, and his schemes are transmitted through the
world system over which Satan, the "god of this world," rules

(2 Corinthians 4:4). His highly structured demonic army purposes to devastate the lives of those who are unprepared.

Pastor Steven Cole expressed it this way:

> If you're ignorant of his schemes, the devil will be able to take advantage of you. His schemes invariably use cunning and deception. He often works through secular culture, to carry us downstream with the prevailing ideas of the day. In our day, many Christians are deceived by the ideas of postmodernism, which asserts that there are no absolute truths in the spiritual or moral realms (except for the absolute that there are no absolutes!). Satan launches repeated attacks on the credibility of Scripture, whether through evolution or by attacking the person of Christ. Satan lures us into sin by portraying it as pleasurable and by hiding its consequences. He uses discouragement, pride, selfishness, the love of money, lust, and many other traps to lure us away from the Lord. To stand firm against the enemy, we must understand his schemes.[1]

Attempting to single-handedly tear down the fortresses we built and fortified over the years is futile. We need Weapons of Divine Power to demolish them. No amount of human effort will successfully destroy the strongholds that Satan helped you build because he has a vested interest in wanting them to remain standing.

The Armor of God

When we choose to put on the armor of God, we have access to many Weapons of Divine Power described in Ephesians 6:13-18. Although ridiculed by the world, these Weapons of Divine Power are greatly feared by demonic powers. When we fight with truth, righteousness, peace, faith, salvation, the Word of God, and prayer, no spiritual forces of evil can stand against us. They are mighty for breaking down Satan's deceptions and for demolishing strongholds and prideful human arguments. If we are going to win our spiritual battles, we must wise up to Satan's schemes and prepare in advance for victory. I have discussed most of these weapons in one form or another, but this is a good place to briefly review them.

Belt of TRUTH: (Ephesians 6:14, John 3:21; 4:24; 16:13; 17:17; 18:37, Philippians 4:8, 1Timothy 2:3-7)

Then you will know the truth, and the truth will set you free. (John 8:32)

The belt of truth held the sheath for the soldier's sword and kept his breastplate in place. It also prevented his tunic from getting tangled up while battling the enemy. Truth is essential in keeping our thoughts and attitudes in their proper perspective so Satan doesn't trip us up.

Satan's first ploy in the Garden of Eden was to cast doubt on God's Word. Truth upholds the very word of God (the sword) and helps us to view our righteousness (the breastplate) correctly. It teaches us right from wrong and prevents us from being deceived by the world's tolerance of sin and rejection of moral absolutes.

Truth tells us that we always have a choice. We can stumble in the futility of our minds, or we can walk boldly in the truth. If we choose the former, Satan will deceive us. Jesus consistently affirmed the foundational significance of truth.

The Belt of Truth also refers to our truthfulness or integrity. When we deliberately deceive others we give Satan a foothold in our lives. We are described as being new creatures in Jesus Christ (2 Corinthians 5:17). We are called to be truthful people—free from hypocrisy and deception—as we make our stand against Satan's schemes.

Breastplate of RIGHTEOUSNESS: (Ephesians 6:14, Psalm 5:12, John 5:24, Romans 3:22; 10:4, 2 Corinthians 5:17-21, 1 Peter 3:12)

*God made him who had no sin to be sin for us, so that in him
we might become the righteousness of God.
(2 Corinthians 5:21)*

The breastplate of righteousness guarded the soldier's vital organs.
Likewise, it protects us from the ravages of sin. Righteousness is
God's gift to every believer through the shed blood of Jesus Christ.
It is maintained totally by Him and can never be taken from us.
We are accountable to reflect His righteousness by refusing to allow
sin to reign in our lives. This is possible only as we walk closely with
the Holy Spirit (Romans 8:5-6; 12-13; Galatians 5:16). As we do,
Christ's righteousness produces a righteous character within us.
Our failure to cooperate with the Holy Spirit leaves us vulnerable
to the enemy.

Christ places a high premium on righteousness, for He lists it as
one of the essentials for blessing and happiness (Matthew 5:6).

The Shoes of PEACE: (Ephesians 6:15, Numbers 6:24-26,
Psalm 29:11; 133:1, Proverbs 16:7, Isaiah 54:10, Matthew 5:9,
Luke 2:14, Acts 10:36, James 3:17)

*Therefore, since we have been justified through faith, we have
peace with God through our Lord Jesus Christ, through whom
we have gained access by faith into this grace in which we now
stand. (Romans 5:1-2)*

Paul describes a soldier's footwear as "the gospel of peace" to be
used in crushing our enemy (Romans 16:20). If we are going to
stand our ground against Satan, we must be convinced that we have
peace with God through His Son, Jesus Christ. In Scripture, Satan
is referred to as the accuser of the brethren (Revelation 12:10). But
Christ is our advocate who lives to intercede for us (Hebrews 7:25).
We must never forget that, through Christ, we have peace with God.
Otherwise, Satan will overwhelm us with false guilt by reminding
us of our past sins.

We are called, as much as possible, to be at peace with others (Romans 12:17-18). Satan delights in using our anger, bitterness, and unforgiving spirit to rob us of our peace. In a world where fear is a greater reality than faith, God has given us the awesome privilege to live out the gospel of peace and to point others to its source.

The Shield of FAITH: (Ephesians 6:16, Mark 9:23, Luke 17:6, John 14:12; 20:29, 1 Corinthians 2:5, Galatians 2:16, Galatians 5:5, Ephesians 2:8, Philippians 4:13, 2 Timothy 1:13, Hebrews 10:22-23; 11:1; 11:6; 12:2)

In him and through faith in him we may approach God with freedom and confidence. (Ephesians 3:12)

When the enemy attacks, we are to shield ourselves from Satan's lies and temptations with the appropriate truth from God's Word. Intellectual truth will do little to help unless we first transfer it to our hearts where it can be lived out as faith in our daily lives.

Although faith is a gift of God, we do bear a responsibility to cultivate it by continually exposing our hearts and minds to the Word of God (Romans 10:17). Our toughest battles will always be about issues of faith. God wants us to trust Him by choosing to believe His truth rather than the enemy's lies.

The Helmet of SALVATION: (Ephesians 6:17, 1 Corinthians 6:11, Ephesians 1:4, 2 Corinthians 5:21, John 10:27-30, 1 Thessalonians 5:8-10, 1 Timothy 2:5, 1 Peter 1:5, 9)

Salvation is found in no one else, for there is no other name under heaven given to men by which we must be saved. (Acts 4:12)

Satan attempts to destroy a believer's assurance of salvation through doubt and discouragement. To stand strong we must remember that our salvation is eternally protected. We belong to the Lord and are securely positioned with Christ in the heavenly realms (Ephesians 2:6). The helmet covers the past, present, and future aspects of our salvation.

Justification (past) occurred when we accepted Christ as our savior. At that point, all of our sins past, present, and future were removed from us and transferred to Christ (1 Peter 3:18). Sanctification (present) is a lifelong process in which we are to participate as we live under control of the Holy Spirit. As we grow in faith and learn to submit our will to God, we become less worldly (Philippians 1:6; 2:12-13). Glorification (future) refers to that wonderful day in the future when we will have a new body, free from sin and all corruption (Romans 8:17, Philippians 3:21).

When we stumble, Satan is right there to tell us that we have blown it. His subtle lies confuse our minds and cause us to forget about God's grace. God's Word assures us that our salvation is secure because we are sealed forever with the Holy Spirit (Ephesians 1:13-14).

The Sword of the Spirit…the WORD OF GOD: (Ephesians 6:17, Psalm 1:2, Jeremiah 23:29, Matthew 7:24, Luke 11:28, John 5:39; 17:17, Acts 17:11, Romans 16:26, Colossians 3:16, 2 Timothy 3:15, 1 Peter 2:2)

For the word of God is living and active. Sharper than any double-edged sword, it penetrates even to dividing soul and spirit, joints and marrow; it judges the thoughts and attitudes of the heart. (Hebrews 4:12)

The sword symbolizes specific passages of Scripture that the Spirit brings to mind when we need them. It is different from the other pieces of armor in that we can use it defensively or offensively.

When Christ was alone in the desert, Satan appeared to Jesus and tempted Him three times. Christ defended himself by quoting specific verses of Scripture that applied directly to the situation (Matthew 4:4,

7, 10). The Bible encourages us to do likewise when the enemy comes against us.

We use the sword as an offensive attack against Satan when we share the good news of the gospel with others. I am using the Sword offensively right now as I write to you.

As with a real sword, it is effective and deadly to the enemy, but we can severely injure ourselves or others if we handle it improperly. The enemy is skilled at twisting Scripture and using it as a means to further darken our minds. This can happen when we take Scripture out of context, misapply a promise, claim a "truth" by focusing on a single verse rather than taking the whole counsel of God into consideration, etc. Wielding a sword takes a lot of practice and skill; so does handling the Word of God. To avoid injury we must study it diligently and humbly seek guidance and insight from the Holy Spirit (2 Timothy 2:15; 3:16-17).

God calls us to know and understand His Word. We can be sure the enemy will tempt us into thinking we know better than God when it comes to handling our circumstances. We need to wield the Sword of the Spirit correctly so that when the serpent hisses in our ear, "Did God really say?..." we will be able to forcefully reply, "It is written!"

Other Spiritual Weapons

PRAYERS and REQUESTS: (Ephesians 6:18, Psalm 18:6, Proverbs 15:29, Isaiah 65:24, Luke 11:13, Romans 8:26, Ephesians 2:18; 3:20, Philippians 4:6, Hebrews 4:16, James 1:5-7; 5:16, 1 Peter 3:12, 1 John 5:14-15)

Call to me and I will answer you and tell you great and unsearchable things you do not know. (Jeremiah 33:3)

Sincere prayer is a beautiful expression of our faith and trust in God as we acknowledge our utter dependence on Him. While not a part of the actual armor that Paul describes, prayer is most definitely a Weapon of Divine Power . By staying in communication with God, we will know how to deal decisively with the enemy. Jesus taught His disciples how to pray (Matthew 6:5-13), and many of His teachings included lessons on the diligence of prayer (Luke 18:1-8), which He exemplified through His own prayer life.

As the apostle Peter found out (Matthew 26:41), prayer is especially needful when struggling with temptation. When we take the time to prepare ourselves spiritually through prayer, we will not give in to temptation that will later break our heart. Good intentions are not enough. When we trust in the weakness of our flesh, we will surely fail.

PRAISE: (Philippians 4:4, 8; Hebrews 13:15, Psalm 33:2; 47:1; 63:3-4; 66:1; 107:8-9; 148, Daniel 2:20; 4:37, Luke 1:46; 2:20, Revelation 4:8; 11:16-17)

Praise the LORD, O my soul; all my inmost being, praise his holy name. Praise the LORD, O my soul, and forget not all his benefits. (Psalm 103:1-2)

Praise is giving glory and honor to God; it is worshiping Him for who He is and what He has done. It is our way of expressing joy and deep satisfaction in the person of God. Praise may be manifest in numerous ways, such as worshiping together through psalms, hymns, and spiritual songs, or singing and making music in our hearts to the Lord (Ephesians 5:19). It may consist of boasting or acclaiming His mighty works so that others will hear and rejoice (Psalm 34:1-3). It may be an expression of the love that spills from our souls us as we silently pray to Him. Praise is most often thought of as a corporate act of worship (Psalm 79:13, Acts 2:46-47), but we can certainly praise Him in private (Psalm 104:34).

Do you see why praise is such a strong weapon against the enemy? Satan's downfall was pride. He wanted to make himself like the

Most High and sought to raise his throne above God's (Isaiah 14:13-14). Instead he was expelled from heaven and will one day be cast into the lake of fire (Revelation 20:10). There is nothing he hates more than hearing God's people bring praise and adoration to their Creator. He simply will not hang around to listen. A powerful way to put Satan on the run is to fill our lives with praises to God.

THANKFULNESS: (Philippians 4:6, Psalm 28:6-7; 75:1, Luke 17:16, 2 Corinthians 9:15, Ephesians 5:19-20, Colossians 1:3; 1:12; 3:15; 1Timothy 1:12, Hebrews 12:28, James 1:17)

Be joyful always; pray continually; give thanks in all circumstances, for this is God's will for you in Christ Jesus. (1 Thessalonians 5:16-18)

Thanksgiving is more than a demonstration of gratitude for all God has done; it is an attitude, a posture, a way of life! The grateful heart recognizes that every good and perfect gift comes from God (James 1:17). We should always have a grateful heart for the many spiritual blessings that have come to us through Christ (Ephesians 1:3) and remember to thank Him for the day-to-day blessings He brings into our lives or the lives of those we love. A grateful heart is also our greatest defense against selfishness, envy, bitterness, discontent, and self-pity.

When we remember all that Jesus has done for us and in us, it is fitting to address every prayer with thanksgiving. While gratitude results in generosity, a lack of gratitude can open the door for Satan, giving him the power to darken our hearts and our minds (Romans 1:21).

Cultivating Your Faith: Four Steps to Freedom

Have you struggled with persistent unwanted thoughts that weaken your faith and cause you to become discouraged, fearful, angry, discontent, or fixated on some unhealthy desire? Perhaps you are besieged with a lot of worrisome thoughts. You are not alone. Many of us are unable to stay calm or think clearly because we are full of fear and anxiety, either over events that may happen or things we believe to be imminent. I have known people who are compulsive worriers; it has become a way of life for them (*stronghold*). They even worry when there *seems* to be nothing to worry about, taking it as an indication that they are not seeing the whole picture. When confronted they maintain that worrying is a good thing; it keeps them on their toes and ready for disaster (*argument*). They further assert that since no one else (*including God*) is going to rescue them from calamity, they must remain alert and expectant (*pretention: self-sufficiency and independence from God*).

Perhaps you have identified one or more strongholds that have negatively affected your ability to trust God. Our God is a God of order and purpose (1 Colossians 14:40, Ephesians 1:11), so you can know that He has an orderly plan for helping you conquer any stronghold. Let's look at some practical steps you can take as you use Weapons of Divine Power to demolish strongholds, arguments, and every pretension that sets itself up against the knowledge of God.

(1) Admit the truth—our thoughts have been destructive

We can't begin the process of demolishing strongholds or removing destructive thoughts from our minds until we first recognize their existence and decide to take a stand against them. The enemy is vicious; he delights in taking advantage of normal, healthy thoughts and desires in order to twist them into ungodly wants or obsessions. In the previous chapter I demonstrated how the anticipation and excitement of having a vacation home in the woods took on a life of its own as it competed with God for the number one spot in my life.

Because they may begin as positive and wholesome, strongholds are not always easy to recognize. By failing to take every thought captive, we unwittingly invite Satan, the father of lies, to warp our beliefs, attitudes, and patterns of thinking. Our sense of reality may become so distorted that negative, unhealthy thoughts seem true, good, or realistic.

(2) Call out to God—Prayer

Calling out to God for wisdom, insight, and strength is the single most important thing we can do. God is our loving Father, and He desires for us to acknowledge those things that have an unhealthy hold over us. When we admit our dependency on Him and express our willingness to trust Him by crying out for help, He promises to come to our aid (Jeremiah 33:3, Matthew 7:9-11). You may know exactly what holds you captive, but if you cannot identify those things that are stealing your peace and eroding your faith, ask God to give you understanding. Ask Him to reveal the rationalizations you use to keep them in place. He is most eager to remove the controlling power from our thoughts so they will no longer have authority over our lives. Getting control of our thoughts doesn't happen overnight. Keep praying and asking God to help you. God has graciously given us the weapon of prayer; we are admonished to use it!

(3) Repent and confess

We studied repentance and confession in the previous chapter, so I will be brief. We learned about the dangers of mocking God in willful disobedience. Likewise, by stubbornly engaging in wrong thinking and refusing to surrender our thought lives to God, He can give us over to our desires (Romans 1:28-32, 1 Corinthians 5:5, 1 Timothy 1:20). Are you willing to come to a place where you can call your stronghold a sin? Do you understand why God would consider your controlling thoughts sinful?

Worry is a good example. Worrying is against God's nature and most certainly not His will for our lives. Worrying is a faith killer because it distrusts God's willingness or ability to provide for our needs and calls into question God's wisdom, sovereignty, and power. It is harmful to us physically, emotionally, and spiritually. God's

Word calls us to stop justifying our reasons for worrying and our grounds for passively allowing such destructive thoughts to flourish in the soil of our minds (Matthew 6:25-34, Philippians 4:6).

Confession helps get our faith back on track as we demonstrate to God that we are ready to trust Him. As you confess, be certain to put on the breastplate of righteousness, the shoes of peace, and the helmet of salvation. As we lay ourselves open to the Spirit of truth, He will work to cleanse our hearts from the lies that have enslaved us.

(4) Replace lies with the truth

Recognizing and discarding the lies we have accepted into our minds is an important step in taking every thought captive, but there is more to it. Jesus told a story that illustrates my point. Read Luke 11:24-26.

Why did the evil spirit come back with seven others? Sadly, the man had not replaced the void with something godly. Likewise, when we purge lies and other destructive thoughts from our mind, we must be careful not to leave our "house" empty. Such a state leaves our mind vulnerable to thoughts that are even worse than what had originally plagued us.

Have you ever tried to take an unwanted thought captive by saying to yourself, "I must stop thinking that!"? What happens a moment later? The same troublesome thought comes back, often more vehemently than ever.

Remember Nick? As motivated as he was to create diamonds, he could not force his mind to lock out images of purple during the crucial steps. Telling yourself not to think destructive thoughts, especially thoughts charged with emotion, does not work. You must replace them with healthy, truthful thoughts.

You put your belt of truth on in step one. Now it's time to take the sword of the Spirit out of its sheath and hold the shield of faith high.

Did you read the introduction to this book? If not, please take a few minutes to do so because my story will give you a concrete example of how to take every thought captive using the Word of God. When I lost my job, I couldn't control the fearful thoughts that tormented me day and night. Only as I replaced my destructive thoughts with the healing words of Scripture did the peace of God return to my soul.

We must begin exchanging deception for truth. God will not free us from our stronghold until we've adopted the mind of Christ on this issue (1 Corinthians 2:16). To do this you must go to the source of truth—His Word—in order to determine the truth about your specific stronghold. Inundate your mind with it until you see it as truth and accept it into your heart.

Using a topical Bible or Bible software, search for passages related to your stronghold. Don't just look up one or two verses that pertain to your area of concern. Take in the full counsel of God and study this stronghold in light of the surrounding text. Satan loves to twist Scripture, so don't make it easy for him. Mark or write down the various Scripture references so you can easily find them again.

In noting the various aspects of the stronghold, it will be very helpful to study the lives of those who had similar struggles. How did this stronghold begin in their lives? What were the consequences? Did they seek repentance? If so, how did God respond to them? Appendix B contains numerous examples of Old Testament mentors and role models and the lessons they teach. I strongly urge you to consult it.

Finally, look up passages that tell of God's unfailing compassion, forgiveness, and grace. You will find a multitude!

As you re-read these passages, certain ones will speak to your heart. Write down these verses along with their citations on note cards that you can carry with you.

I can't emphasize enough how important it is for us to carry God's Word around in our heads as well as our hearts. Memorizing Scripture and repeating it often will do much to counteract the nagging thoughts that can trouble our mind. At this point you may be thinking about Jesus' warning about vain repetitious words (Matthew 6:7). We should never engage in meaningless babble or repeat the same words over and over like a magic incantation. But this activity is different for two reasons: First, the point of memorizing Scripture is to drive the *meaning* of the words deep into our minds. Second, motive is important to God. He will honor what we are doing if our purposes are pure. God is pleased by our desire to carry His Word within us so that we can defend ourselves against the attacks of Satan or use it as a witnessing tool with others (Matthew 28:18-20, Ephesians 1:13).

As we sleep our thoughts are especially vulnerable to Satan's attacks. In the beginning days of my trial (as described in the Introduction), I woke up each morning anxious and fearful because I had been worrying the entire night. After deciding to take my thoughts captive I did two things before going to sleep. First, I asked God to guard my thoughts as I slept (Isaiah 26:3, Philippians 4:7). Second, I lived out the words of Psalm 63:6: "On my bed I remember you; I think of you through the watches of the night." As I waited for sleep to come I repeated the Scripture that I had been memorizing. All night long, even when asleep, the comforting Psalms spoke to my mind. If I awoke during the night, I would remember God as I called Scripture verses to mind. God faithfully stood watch over my mind in its weak and vulnerable state. I never woke up fearful or anxious. He will do the same for you too. God's promise is sure; His Word will not return void to us (Isaiah 55:11).

The enemy is fierce, but God has given us a multitude of spiritual weapons with which to defend ourselves and put Satan on the run. As much as we might want to, we cannot stay neutral in this spiritual battle. The Bible describes Satan as ruler of this dark world, so until God crushes him under foot, we are trespassing on his turf. Our very existence offends him greatly, and he is infuriated by our allegiance to God. Yet we have no reason to fear him, for Satan is a defeated enemy. In His own good time, our Commander will deliver to him a deadly blow. In the meantime, God calls us to put on His armor and stand our ground.

Prayer Time

All Powerful Father,

Thank You for providing me with powerful spiritual weapons so that I can demolish those things that set themselves up against You. Show me how to develop a steadfast mind that is focused on You. Protect my mind and guard me from troublesome thoughts. Teach me to rest on Your promises. I invite You to be Lord of my mind. I pray these things in the name of Jesus Christ, whose precious blood has cleansed me from every transgression—past, present, and future! Amen.

Cultivating Your Garden of Faith

Get It Straight:

1. In what ways is the peace of God different from the peace that the world offers?

2. What six pieces make up the armor of God? Describe each piece and explain how it works to protect us.

3. How are prayer, praise, and thanksgiving helpful during spiritual warfare?

4. Look up the verses included in the description of each weapon. What other things do these verses tell you about the particular weapon?

Head to Heart:

1. Can you remember a time when God kept you in His peace despite difficult circumstances? If so, consider sharing this experience with others. If you cannot recall such a time, review the characteristics of a steadfast mind and ask God to help you learn how to rest your thoughts upon Him in good times and in bad. Seek encouragement from others.

2. Can you recall a disappointing or painful experience that you can now look back on and honestly give thanks to God for? In what ways does this remembrance make it easier to trust that God is using your current difficulties for your good?

3. Spend time now reciting the memory Scripture verses that you have learned. Which ones speak to your heart the most? (If you have not already done so, write the citations to these verses on a small note card to carry with you. Recite the associated passages often.)

4. What lies and accusations does the enemy commonly fire at us? Write some down, then look up promises or teachings from Scripture to thwart them. Share them with others for encouragement.

You and God:

1. Are you aware of any strongholds or controlling thoughts that you need to take captive? If so, can you identify the arguments and pretensions that maintain them? Are you willing to apply the four steps to freedom to one or more of them?

2. God asks us to "give thanks in all circumstances" (1 Thessalonians 5:18). What is currently troubling you? Are you willing to thank God *in advance* for the good things He will bring out of your struggles? If not, what thoughts are stopping you? Are they from God? Do you need to repent of them?

3. Remember the list of blessings from chapter eight I asked you to save? Thank God and praise Him for every item on the list. Now add more items to each category in your list.

4. Which piece(s) of spiritual armor have you neglected to put on in the past? What was the result of not being prepared?

Scripture Memory

Though the mountains be shaken and the hills be removed, yet my unfailing love for you will not be shaken nor my covenant of peace be removed, says the LORD, who has compassion on you. (Isaiah 54:10)

Personal Thoughts:

_____

_____

_____

_____

_____

Appendix A
Apologetic Bibliographies

Ankerberg, John and Dillon Burroughs. *Taking a Stand for the Bible: Today's Leading Experts Answer Critical Questions about God's Word.* Eugene, OR: Harvest House Publishers, 2009.

Archer, Gleason L. Jr. *New International Encyclopedia of Bible Difficulties.* Grand Rapids, MI: Zondervan, 2001.

Boyd, Gregory A. *Jesus Under Siege.* Wheaton, IL: Victor Books, 1995.

Ewen, Pamela Binnings. *Faith on Trial.* Nashville: Broadman & Holman Publishers, 1999.

Geisler, Norman L. and Ronald M. Brooks. *When Skeptics Ask: A Handbook on Christian Evidences.* Grand Rapids, MI: Baker Books, 2008.

Habermas, Gary R. and Michael R. Licona. *The Case for the Resurrection of Jesus.* Grand Rapids, MI: Kregel Publications, 2004.

Haley, John W. *Alleged Discrepancies of the Bible.* New Kensington, PA: Whitaker House Publishers, 2003.

Hanegraaff, Hank. *Fatal Flaws: What Evolutionists Don't Want You to Know.* Nashville: W Publishing Group, 2006.

Hanegraaff, Hank. *The Face that Demonstrates the Farce of Evolution.* Nashville: Thomas Nelson, 2001.

Little, Paul E. and James F. Nyquist. *Know Why You Believe.* Downers Grove, IL: InterVarsity, 2008.

McDowell, Josh. *A Ready Defense*. Nashville: Thomas Nelson, 1990.

McDowell, Josh. *Evidence for Christianity*. Nashville: Thomas Nelson, 2006.

McDowell, Josh and Sean McDowell. *More Than a Carpenter*. Wheaton, IL: Tyndale House, 2009.

McDowell, Josh. *The New Evidence That Demands a Verdict*. Nashville: Thomas Nelson, 1999.

Strobel, Lee. *The Case for Christ: A Journalist's Personal Investigation of the Evidence for Jesus*. Grand Rapids, MI: Zondervan, 1998.

Strobel, Lee. *The Case for a Creator: A Journalist Investigates Scientific Evidence That Points Toward God*. Grand Rapids, MI: Zondervan, 2004

Strobel, Lee. *The Case for Faith: A Journalist Investigates the Toughest Objections to Christianity*. Grand Rapids, MI: Zondervan, 2000.

Strobel, Lee. *The Case for the Real Jesus: A Journalist Investigates Current Attacks on the Identity of Christ*. Grand Rapids, MI: Zondervan, 2007.

Appendix B

Old Testament Mentors

Here is an opportunity for you to get an in-depth look at the Old Testament mentors and what they teach us. The references to their life stories are shown below. The Old Testament vicariously teaches us many valuable life-lessons. The Bible is filled with both sages and fools along with those who are a little of both. By walking with them for a while, we can learn to avoid costly mistakes that would otherwise oppress us, perhaps for a lifetime. We can also gain rich insights that will give us hope, strengthen our faith, and teach us how to respond rightly to God.

For everything that was written in the past was written to teach us, so that through endurance and the encouragement of the Scriptures we might have hope. (Romans 15:4)

The references to their life stories are shown after their names. These references in many cases are not exhaustive but should give the reader a good understanding about the mentor's life, his or her successes and failures. The specific lessons they teach, as described here, are displayed in ***bold italic*** print.

Following is a small sampling of the many lessons God's righteous Old Testament servants are waiting to teach us.

- Abraham's life demonstrates that we must sometimes give up our comfort and security in order to follow His leading. Blessings and rewards are found only in obedience. (Genesis 12–25) // (***Genesis 12:1-7; 13:14-17; 15; 21:1-7; 22***)

- Joseph's life richly illustrates that God works all things together for the good of those who trust in Him. (Genesis 37, 39–50) // (***Genesis 50:19-21***)

• Through Moses we see how God breaks, prepares, restores, and uses frail people to accomplish great purposes. (Exodus–Deuteronomy) // (***Exodus 2:11–4:17; 6:28–7:7; 14***)

• Joshua encourages us to look beyond our fears—past challenging circumstances—and make a choice to trust in God and serve Him alone. (Exodus 17; 24; 32–33; Numbers 11; 13–14; 26–27; 32; 34,Deuteronomy 1; 3; 31–32; 34; Joshua, Judges 2) // (***Numbers 14:1-9; 14:26-30, Joshua 24:14-15***)

• From Rahab we learn that God works through those who are faithful regardless of their sinful past. (Joshua 2; 6; Matthew 1:5) // (***Joshua 2; 6:15-25, Matthew 1:5***)

• Ruth teaches us about loyalty and commitment in relationships. (Ruth, Matthew 1:5) //(***Ruth 1:16-18; 2:8-11***)

• Hannah helps us to realize that God hears and answers our prayers. (**1 Samuel 1–2**)

• David inspires us to quickly confess our sins to God and seek after Him with all our hearts. (1 Samuel 16–27, 2 Samuel, 1 Kings 1–2) // (***2 Samuel 12:9-24, Psalm 32, Psalm 51***)

• Elijah tells us that God is close no matter how lonely and discouraged we feel. God will gladly speak to us if we are willing to listen for His gentle whisper. (1 Kings 17–19; 21, 2 Kings 1–2) // (***1 Kings 19***)

• Esther shows us how God has a purpose for the circumstances in which He places us. (***Esther***)

• From Job we learn much about patience, perseverance, and integrity through suffering. Knowing God and having Him by our side is supremely better than understanding the reasons for our afflictions. (Job) // (***Job 1:20-22; 42***)

• Isaiah helps us realize that our lives will never change until we come to see God as holy. (2 Kings 19–20, Isaiah 6:1) // (*Isaiah 6:1*)

The sinful and foolish actions of God's Old Testament people also help us to recognize hazardous pits before we fall into them:

• Jacob shows us what happens when we deceive others and rely on our own resources rather than seeking God's help. (Genesis 25; 27–35; 37; 42–50) (*Genesis 27; 29:14-30; 37:19-36*)

• Esau advises us to consider the long-range consequences when faced with important decisions. (Genesis 25–28; 32–33; 35–36 Hebrews 12:16-17) // (*Genesis 25:27-34; 27:1-40*)

• Moses demonstrates the consequences of failing to deal with one's anger. (Exodus–Deuteronomy) // (*Exodus 2:11-15; 32:18-20, Numbers 20:8-12*)

• The desert-dwelling Israelites reveal how God ultimately deals with complaining, stiff-necked, unbelieving people. Prolonged disobedience will keep us from experiencing God's promises. (Exodus—Deuteronomy) // (*Exodus 15:22–17:7; 32; Numbers 10:11–14:45; 16; 20:1-13*)

• From Samson we learn the consequences of being controlled by our passions and recognize the importance of placing our trust in those who are trustworthy. (Judges 13–16) // (*Judges 16*)

• Through King Saul we observe the severe consequences of disobedience and jealousy. (1 Samuel 9–31) // (*1 Samuel 13; 15; 18–19:1-3*)

• From David's life we see what happens when we fail to deal decisively with our children's sinful behavior. We also learn that forgiveness does not remove the consequences of sin. (1Samuel 16–27; 2 Samuel, 1Kings 1–2) // (*2 Samuel 12:9-12; 13; 15:13-16; 16:20-22; 18:33–19:4*)

🌱

- Solomon teaches us that we must be careful whom we marry; unbelieving spouses can affect our loyalty to God. Finding meaning and satisfaction in life apart from God is a vain pursuit. (2 Samuel 12:24–1Kings 1–43) // (*1 Kings 11:1-6, Ecclesiastes*)

- King Uzziah's life reveals how easy it is to become prideful when we meet with success and how tragedy ensues when we fail to deal with our pride. Uzziah is also called Azariah (2 Kings 15; 2 Chronicles 26) // (*2 Chronicles 26:16-23*)

- Jonah teaches us that obedience to God is infinitely better than running away from Him. (*Jonah*)

☙

Appendix C

Guided Prayers

Chapter 1: Is Your Belief System Working For You?

Heavenly Father, as I begin this personal study on faith-building, help me to be diligent. Open my heart and my mind; give me the courage to honestly and accurately assess where I am on this bumpy road of faith. Disclose areas in my life that I have not yet entrusted to Your loving care, and give me the courage to turn all my struggles over to You. Reveal any inconsistencies in my life—especially things I claim to believe but don't put into practice.

Your Word says that Christ came to give me an abundant life. Help me to understand what that means on a very personal level, because I truly want to experience the joy, peace and assurance that You have for me even in difficult times.

I don't merely want to have intellectual knowledge about You; it is wholly my desire to develop a deeper, more intimate love for You. I want to be able to trust in You fully, even when I can't see the path in front of me. Please help me in my quest, for I know that I cannot accomplish it on my own.

Thank You for the measure of faith You have already given me. I ask You now to use this study to further cultivate it into a faith that flourishes.

Father, Your Word says, "And we can be confident that he will listen to us whenever we ask him for anything in line with his will. And if we know he is listening when we make our requests, we can be sure that he will give us what we ask for" (1 John 5:14-15 NLT). Lord, I am greatly reassured by these verses, for I know that I am praying in Your will at this very moment.

All these things I pray in Jesus' name. Amen.

(Are there parts of this prayer that you can't pray just yet? God understands; don't be discouraged. Talk to Him as you are able, and He will meet you where you are).

Chapter 2: What is Faith?

Dear Heavenly Father,

I come before You with a heart and mind that sincerely want to know you. You have asked us to love you not only with our hearts and souls and strength, but also with our minds! I am grateful that you welcome my honest doubts and difficult questions. As I take this faith journey, I ask that you make yourself known to me in a very real way. Fill me with your assurance and sweep away any destructive doubts that dwell within me.

Father, I live in a culture that believes that truth is relative, but this is a lie of Satan. For Jesus boldly asserted that He is the truth, that your Word is the truth, that we are made holy by the truth, that we will know the truth and that the truth will set us free. Truth, therefore, is the anchor that faith holds fast to, for faith that is not based on knowledge, truth, and understanding will surely crumble. Lord, I come in earnest seeking the truth and the reassurance of Your truth. Therefore, by Your truth, I ask you now to set me free from worry, doubt, and fear.

Enable me to understand the role my faith plays as I walk with you. Teach me to keep my faith strong and healthy through knowledge and understanding rather than foolish ignorance. Your Word says that without faith we cannot please You. I ask You, therefore, to help me make a conscious decision to set aside my doubts and be willing to commit to whatever it is that you have for me.

Help me be a faithful witness. I am instructed to always be prepared to give an answer to everyone who asks me to give the reason for my hope.

You have called me to take up the shield of faith, a faith that is overflowing with passion, commitment, and good works; help me to respond!

I pray these things in the One who is the very essence of Truth, My Lord and Savior, Jesus Christ.

Chapter 3: Can You Trust the Bible?

Dear Heavenly Father,

Thank You for giving us Your eternal, perfect Word of Truth! When I realize how powerfully it has endured the test of time, I stand amazed and truly grateful. Thank You for breathing Your very words into the minds of men who willingly responded to Your call. Thank You for preserving Your Word throughout the ages in spite of evil men who deliberately sought to destroy it. Thank You for raising up devout and courageous men who faithfully copied and protected your Holy Word, even to death, so that I, centuries later, could come to know You!

At times I am perplexed when I read the Scriptures, because the words are puzzling to me. On other occasions I am troubled because its message is difficult to accept. Precious Spirit of Truth, I ask You to teach and guide me into all truth so that I may understand and receive those things You wish to reveal to me. Help me to be receptive to Your promptings even when my flesh wants to resist. Strengthen my faith and convict me of any skepticism residing in my heart. Challenge me to study the Word diligently so that I may correctly judge the things that I hear, holding fast to the truth and dispelling all deception.

Father, you sent your Son to testify to the truth. Our culture tries to strip truth away and replace it with a "whatever-seems-right-to-me" philosophy. Yet Jesus said that everyone on the side of truth listens to Him. Help me not only to recognize the voice of Truth, but to listen and receive it with joy! You have asked me to love You not only with all of my heart, soul, and strength, but also with my mind. I am encouraged, therefore, when I observe accusations that have been leveled against the Bible silenced in the light of new archeological discovery. My faith is strengthened when I study the amazing fulfillment of prophecy.

Help me do my best to present myself to You as an approved and unashamed worker—one who correctly handles the word of truth (2 Timothy 2:15). Help my life to always reflect the truth of Your Word. I pray these things in the One who is the very essence of truth, My Lord and Savior, Jesus Christ.

Chapter 4: What Your Faith Means to God

O sovereign God, Creator of all that exists,

You are marvelous beyond comparison. "When I consider your heavens, the work of your fingers," I am amazed and awed by Your glory and Your majesty. Who am I that You are mindful of me? How is it that You call me Your "masterpiece," Your "treasured possession"? You know me intimately—the dark secrets of my heart, my rebellious ways, the pride and selfishness that I harbor deep inside—and yet You have chosen to love me with an everlasting love, and even more astonishing, you have invited me to enter into an intimate relationship with You!

Father, I confess that my heart grows cold at times. Please help me to hear and respond to Your voice so that I never become hardened by sin's deceitfulness or waver in my faith to the point where I can no longer hear Your voice, accept Your wisdom, or take hold of the rich blessings that You have for me.

Lord, I want to believe You with all my heart, but too often I find myself listening to my feelings instead of Your Word. There are times when You seem distant, and I am unable to sense Your presence. Help me to remember, during those dark times, that You are always close to me; indeed, it is You who seek after me! Help me likewise to search for You with all my heart, for You alone deserve my adoration and my praise! As I seek You, I cling not only to the promise that I will I find you, but also to your assurance that I will be blessed in the process.

What an amazing calling! There is no way that I can ever live up to it! But I know that I am not left on my own with such an impossible task. Thank you, Father, for sending Jesus to be the "author and perfecter of our faith." I know it is "Christ in [me]"—the Holy Spirit—who enables me to walk in your ways, thereby bringing You glory. In accordance with Your Word, I ask You to help me grow in my faith. Help me to be a true and faithful witness—one who brings glory and honor to Your name by my actions and words.

I pray these things in Jesus' name. Amen!

Chapter 5: Feeling Let Down by God

Father, You are steadfast and faithful and have promised never to abandon me. Yet I confess that all too often I allow anxiety over my future to dominate my thinking. When my most heartfelt prayers remain unanswered, remind me that Your timing is always perfect. Teach me to wait patiently upon You. In the meantime encourage me to rejoice in today with renewed strength (Isaiah 40:28-31).

Grant me wisdom and understanding that I may be filled with hope. Instill in me a love for Your Word and instruct me how to correctly handle Scripture so that I will not misconstrue

its meaning. Prompt me to seek solutions to life's problems by turning first to the Bible. Life is full of uncertainty. If I try to make sense of tragedies from a worldly perspective, I will surely become cynical, faithless, and hopeless.

Strengthen my trust in You and cultivate in me a faith that flourishes; make my steps secure so that I will not allow the enemy to gain a foothold in my life. Give me wisdom to detect his lies so that I will not be deceived. Help me take every thought captive so that I do not live with a dread of impending doom or with a false sense of security (2 Corinthians 10:3-5). By Your power I resolve not to fear tragedy should it come, for You are my strength and my shield (Psalm 28:7). I will trust You to get me through anything that happens in my life. Not only will I endure heartaches, but I will be triumphant over them.

Lord, You are all-knowing, all-wise and all-powerful. Your goodness and loving-kindness never cease; therefore, I can trust You to use my suffering to bless me as You advance Your glorious purposes. The safest place to be is in the center of Your will; show me how to meet You there.

I pray these things in Jesus Christ, my Rock and my Fortress (Psalm 62:2). Amen!

Chapter 6: What Are You Doing, God?

Father, I confess that I have been dominated by self-focused thinking in the past. Show me how to fix my eyes upon You instead of on my circumstances. Teach me to never give up or allow negative thoughts such as doubt and discouragement to control my thinking. Enable me to endure my trials while holding on to Your promises. I want to put my trust in You no matter what; teach me to persevere.

I know that You created me to be dependent upon You. Help me come to the end of myself. You have always promised to provide for, protect, and bless Your own, and I fall upon that promise now.

God, I know that You are sovereign over all Your creation and that You rule with perfect wisdom and knowledge; You are righteous and just, and Your mercy and compassion are endless. Your Word promises that in all things You work for the good of those who love You and have been called according to Your purpose (Romans 8:28). I, therefore, acknowledge Your good and perfect work in my life. As painful as tragedy is, I know that it is never senseless, meaningless, or unredeemable. While I usually don't understand the pain You have allowed in my life, You have a loving purpose behind every tribulation, and so I chose to trust You in this. Instead of looking for reasons behind my distress, motivate me to seek Your wisdom so I will know how I am to respond to my adversity in a way that brings You glory. Strengthen my faith during trials and use them to draw me closer to Your heart. Help me to learn the lessons You have for me. Use my suffering to create a more Christ-like character within me.

You have promised to go with me into the fire and to deliver me from it at the proper time. I will come through my past, present and future afflictions with a greater sense of peace, joy and hope as I put my trust in You. Enable my faith to flourish not simply in spite of the hardships I have experienced but because of them. In these things I can rejoice as I pray in the name of Jesus Christ, the fourth man in the fire (Daniel 3:24-25). Amen!

Chapter 7: Trusting God When Life Hurts: (It Isn't Fair... I Didn't Do Anything Wrong!)

Father, I come before You today acknowledging that You alone are my healer. There is no emotional pain that is too deep or too long-standing for You to heal.

Show me how to respond to my adversaries in a way that brings You glory. I do not want unforgiveness, bitterness, or cynicism to keep me in bondage or to impede the flow of Your blessings in my life. Your Word says that unforgiveness is disobedience, so I ask You to help me find a way to sweep resentment out of my heart so I can truly forgive those who have wronged me. I can't begin to imagine the pain You suffered for our sins, and yet You forgave! Teach me to follow Your example by forgiving those who have hurt me. When I am tempted to want revenge, remind me that You are righteous and have promised to deal fairly with all people—those who fall upon Your grace as well as those who continue to defy You. Even if I never see the wicked come to shame in this lifetime, I know that justice will be accomplished in Your timing. Let me never utter angry, malicious words that might pull an innocent person into a pit with me.

Strengthen me so that I don't fall prey to the self-pitying lies of the pit! Your Word says that no one can rip me out of Your hands and no one can reverse what You have ordained for me (Isaiah 43:13). By Your sovereign will use my place of pain as a means of delivering me to the exact spot You want me to be.

Thank You for not giving up on me and for meeting me where I am rather than where I should be. Reveal to me what I need to bring to You and show me anything I am currently holding back. Bring me to the point where I am willing to trust You fully in this. Lord, I can't say that I always want to do it Your way, but there is something deep within me that wants to come to the place where that desire is born. Please help me! "Search me, O God, and know my heart; test me and know my anxious thoughts. See if there is any offensive way in me, and lead me in the way everlasting" (Psalm 139:23-24).

I pray these things in the name of my Healer and Deliverer, Jesus Christ.

Chapter 8: Biblical Prosperity

Father, I confess that all too often the desire for "things" has led me on vain pursuits that left me unfilled and unsatisfied. Help me recognize that the emptiness within my soul can only be filled by You. Teach me how to guard my heart against an unhealthy obsession with obtaining money. I want to be rich towards You! Lord, You have placed many worthwhile desires in my heart. Show me how to prevent these desires from turning into a shallow passion for worldly success. As I strive to do my very best, remind me that You do not want me to get ahead by disobeying you. I trust in Your promise to bless me in the things that You have called me to accomplish. Encourage me to be content with the many blessings you have given me. I thank you for your abundant grace and willingness to aid me in every circumstance of life, be it hardship or ease.

Give me a heart like the psalmist's, a heart that longs to obey you, a heart that seeks hard after you. Bring me to a place where I truly love and trust in Your goodness. Help me to accept Your sovereign right to rule over me. In my desire to do Your will, show me how to avoid falling into legalistic thinking or a works-oriented mind-set. I know well that it takes more than self-determination and effort to be victorious over sin and temptation. In the past I always started out so well, but the moment I let up my guard I ended up discouraged and disobedient! Encourage me, instead, to depend daily on the Holy Spirit, for I know that I cannot live a consistently obedient life without His inner presence to guide and strengthen me.

Prompt me to seek You through prayer in all things rather than coming to You as my last remaining option. Teach me to be sensitive to Your will so that my prayers will bring glory and honor to Your name.

I admit that I have often asked You to bless my endeavors rather than seeking Your will for my life. I acknowledge that true blessedness comes as I follow after the things You have planned for me. God, I know that You have awesome plans for me, and I want to see their fulfillment in my life. Show me those things that interfere with Your plans for me. Assist me in turning my fears, worries, doubts, and selfishness over to You, and give me the courage and willingness to cooperate with You. I so want to be fruitful for Your kingdom.

Thank You for blessing me and providing me with everything I need to live a godly and productive life. Help me to grow in my faith so that I will learn to trust You more. I confidently pray these things by the authority granted me in Jesus Christ, Your Beloved Son. Amen!

Chapter 9: Trusting God When Life Hurts (I Can't Believe I Did That!)

Lord, I sometimes find myself in a world of hurt because of poor judgment and foolish behavior. This in turn causes me to fall into a pit of self-pity and self-condemnation. Help me to focus on You rather than on my pain and stir within me the desire to run to You, not from You. Soften my heart and cause me to be genuinely repentant before you now. I am so tired of being controlled by my sinful desires. I want to break free from them, and I can only do it by Your power.

Your Word says that Jesus died for my sins once for all time (1 Peter 3:18) and that there is no condemnation for those who are in Christ Jesus (Romans 8:1). Thank You for loving me in spite of my sins and for promising never to leave me or abandon me (Deuteronomy 31:6). I am comforted in knowing that I can approach the throne of grace with confidence in order to receive mercy and grace in my time of need (Hebrews 4:16). I know that

You still have wonderful plans for me. Guide me back onto the right path that I might fulfill them.

cxototoxo

(If you have committed willful sins or are trapped in addictive behavior): *Father, I am deeply troubled because I have deliberately sinned by _____ (my sin). In my selfishness I cared more about what I wanted than what You wanted. I made light of my sin because I knew you are a loving, forgiving God. Forgive me for showing contempt for the riches of Your kindness, tolerance, and patience. In my blindness I did not realize that it is Your kindness that leads me toward repentance (Romans 2:4). Teach me how to put this callous attitude to death. I have fallen into worldly sorrow instead of true repentance and thus have failed repeatedly to change my behavior. Grant me a repentant heart, for I know that even the ability to repent is a gift from You (2 Timothy 2:25). I don't want my heart to become so hard that I become insensitive to_____ (my sin). Keep me from willful sins; may they not rule over me. I want to be blameless in Your sight (Psalm 19:13).*

(If others have been hurt by your sin): *Father, bring to my mind those who have been hurt by my sin. I want to make things right with_____ (the person I hurt). Give me the desire, courage, integrity and wisdom to do this in a manner that honors You.*

cxototoxo

Forgive me for making excuses or for blaming others. I acknowledge that I have no one to blame but myself. I now confess _____ (my sin) before You and agree with what You have to say about it.

Thank you for your loving discipline. I know it was given for my benefit—so that I would repent and turn to You for healing. I know You will lead me safely through this, and my regret will be transformed into joy. Thank You for sending Your Son to die for my sins so that I could be forgiven and made whole again. Thank

You for restoring my fellowship with You; I pray these things in the name of Jesus Christ, whose precious blood has cleansed me from every transgression—past, present, and future! Amen!

Chapter 10: Taking Every Thought Captive: Battling Discouraging Thoughts

Father, show me how to develop a steadfast mind that is focused on You. Protect my mind and guard me from troublesome thoughts. Teach me to rest on Your promises. I invite You to be Lord of my mind.

Thank You for providing me with powerful spiritual weapons so that I can demolish those things that set themselves up against You. Remind me to put on Your armor daily and teach me how to effectively use the weapons of truth, righteousness, peace, faith, salvation, and the Word against the dark spiritual forces that war against Your beloved children.

I want to develop an attitude of joy, prayerfulness, thanksgiving, and praise. When troubled or tempted by evil, let my first response be to seek You in prayer. Give me a truly grateful heart and help me to be thankful in all circumstances as I trust You to bring joy out of sorrow.

I confess my dependency upon You and call out to You for help against those things that have an unhealthy hold over me. As I seek to cultivate my faith, uproot my strongholds along with the excuses I use to maintain them. Weed out the prideful attitudes that keep them fortified and sow in me a repentant heart. I trust You to cleanse my mind from the lies that have enslaved me.

Father, as I begin this process of self-examination, help me to be honest with both You and myself. Enlighten my mind so that I may identify those things that need to be removed from my life. Reveal strongholds, addictive behaviors, willful disobedience

and areas of repetitive sin that interfere with my fellowship with You. Guide me as I search Your Word for verses relating to the areas of sin in my life. Point me to Scripture that will reveal the truth about my sins and help me accept the truth into my mind and heart so that I am able to see my sin as you see it.

Lord, as I tear down lies, I do not want to leave my "house" empty. Fill my mind with truth from Your Word. There is so much deception surrounding my beliefs about my rebellious behavior, and I can no longer trust what I think or feel. Help me to sort out the truth from the lies so that I may be set free (John 8:32).

When the enemy attacks bring Scripture to mind that will strengthen and comfort me. May I be diligent in studying Your Word. Encourage me to seek guidance and insight from the Holy Spirit. Give me a strong desire to place Your words of life into my mind and help me concentrate as I seek to memorize them.

Protect my mind while I sleep; keep my thoughts centered on You through the watches of the night (Psalm 63:6) so that in the morning I will wake rested and free from the previous day's worry. I pray these things in the name of Him who is able to guard what I have entrusted to Him this day (1 Titus 2:12), my Lord and Savior, Jesus Christ! Amen!

Notes

Chapter 2—What is Faith?

1. Paul E. Little and Marie Little, *Know Why You Believe* (Downers Grove, IL: InterVarsity, 1988), 16-17.

Chapter 3—Can You Trust the Bible?

1. Little and Little, *Know Why You Believe*, 62-63.

2. John Ankerberg, Dillon Burroughs, *Taking a Stand for the Bible* (Eugene, OR: Harvest House Publishers, 2009), 74; Paul Feinberg. "The Meaning of Inerrancy" in *Inerrancy* ed. Norman Geisler (Grand Rapids: Zondervan, 1980), 294.

3. Josh McDowell, *The New Evidence That Demands a Verdict* (Nashville: Thomas Nelson, 1999), 4-6.

4. Henrietta C. Mears, *What the Book Is All About* (Wheaton, IL: Tyndale House, 1987), 13. "What The Book Is All About" is condensed from *What the Bible Is All About*, 1953, 1954, 1960, 1966, 1983 by Gospel Light Publications, Living Bible edition. Copyright 1987 by Tyndale House Publishers.

5. Norman L. Geisler and Ronald M. Brooks, *When Skeptics Ask* (Wheaton, IL: Victor Books, 1990), 158.

6. McDowell, *The New Evidence That Demands a Verdict*, 76; Norman L. Geisler, *Baker Encyclopedia of Christian Apologetics* (Grand Rapids: Baker, 1998), 552.

7. Geisler and Brooks, *When Skeptics Ask*, 157-158

8. Little and Little, *Know Why You Believe*, 75

9. McDowell, *The New Evidence That Demands a Verdict*, 70; Gleason L. Archer, Jr. *A Survey of Old Testament Introduction* (Chicago: Moody Press, 1964, 1974) 23-25

10. Ankerberg and Burroughs, *Taking a Stand for the Bible*, 34, 56-57; McDowell, *The New Evidence That Demands a Verdict*, 34; Norman Geisler, William Nix, *A General Introduction to the Bible* (Chicago: Moody Press, 1971), 238, 357-67. Greek text figures are updated based on recently discovered Geek texts by the Center for the Study of New Testament Manuscripts at www.csntm.org.

11. Ankerberg and Burroughs, *Taking a Stand for the Bible*, 34; McDowell, *The New Evidence That Demands a Verdict*, 37-38; Geisler and Nix, *A General Introduction to the Bible*, 408.

12. Ankerberg and Burroughs, *Taking a Stand for the Bible*, 134-136.

13. Ankerberg and Burroughs, *Taking a Stand for the Bible*, 136. This information was taken from an interview with Dr. Daniel Wallace, professor of New Testament at Dallas Theological Seminary from program two of "The Battle to Dethrone Jesus" on "The John Ankerberg Show," 2007. The video, audio, and/or transcript of this program can be ordered at www.johnankerberg.org.

14. Ankerberg and Burroughs, *Taking a Stand for the Bible*, 58.

15. McDowell, *The New Evidence That Demands a Verdict*, 48-50.

16. McDowell, *The New Evidence That Demands a Verdict*, 53-54, 130-133.

17. McDowell, *The New Evidence That Demands a Verdict*, 5 5-58.

18. Geisler and Brooks, *When Skeptics Ask*, 200.

19. Geisler and Brooks, *When Skeptics Ask*, 201.

20. McDowell, *The New Evidence That Demands a Verdict*, 63; W. M. Ramsay, *St. Paul the Traveler and the Roman Citizen* (Grand Rapids: Baker Book House, 1962), 222.

21. Ankerberg and Burroughs, *Taking a Stand for the Bible*, 148.

22. Little and Little, *Know Why You Believe*, 86; W. F. Albright, "Archaeology and the Religion of Israel," in Howard F. Vos, *An Introduction to Bible Archaeology* (Chicago: Moody Press, n.d.), 121.

23. Geisler and Brooks, *When Skeptics Ask*, 179; Nelson Glueck, *Rivers in the Desert* (New York: Farrar, Strauss and Cudahy, 1959), 136.

24. Ankerberg and Burroughs, *Taking a Stand for the Bible*, 79; J. Barton Payne, *Encyclopedia of Biblical Prophecy* (Grand Rapids: Baker, 1989), 13.

25. Ankerberg and Burroughs, *Taking a Stand for the Bible*, 84-85; Peter Stoner, *Science Speaks: Scientific Proof of the Accuracy of Prophecy and the Bible* (Chicago: Moody Press, 1969), 4.

26. Ankerberg and Burroughs, *Taking a Stand for the Bible*, (p 86); Stoner, *Science Speaks*, 107.

Chapter 4—What Your Faith Means to God

1. W. E. Vine, *The Expanded Vine's Expository Dictionary of New Testament Words*, ed. John R. Kohlenberger III (Minneapolis: Bethany House Publishers, 1984), 766.

Chapter 6—What Are You Doing, God?

1. James MacDonald, *I Really Want To Change…So, Help Me God* (Chicago: Moody Press, 2000), 64.

Chapter 7—Trusting God When Life Hurts: (It Isn't Fair… I Didn't Do Anything Wrong!)

1. Corrie ten Boom with John and Elizabeth Sherrill, *The Hiding Place* (Old Tappan, NJ: Spire Books, 1971), 238.

Chapter 8—Biblical Prosperity

1. Blaise Pascal, W. Bright, *Jesus and the Intellectual* (San Bernardino, CA: Campus Crusade for Christ International Arrowhead Springs, 1968).

2. Robert Morris, *The Blessed Life* (Ventura, CA: Regal Books, 2004), 28.

3. Beth Moore, *Believing God* (Nashville: B&H Publishing Group, 2004), 5.

Chapter 9—Trusting God When Life Hurts: (I Can't Believe I Did That!)

1. Charles W. Colson, *Born Again* (Old Tappan, NJ: Chosen Books, Inc., 1976), 57.

2. Colson, *Born Again*, 71.

3. Colson, *Born Again*, 114.

Chapter 10—Taking Every Thought Captive: Battling Discouraging Thoughts

1. Flagstaff Christian Fellowship, Flagstaff, AZ, October 5, 2008.

Cultivating Faith Ministries
www.cultivatingfaith.com

In our fearful, doubt-driven culture, Cultivating Faith Ministries is devoted to helping Christians overcome fear with faith. Our goal is to encourage Christians as they learn to place their trust in God and His Word, recognize God's faithfulness in their lives, and discover a loving God whose plans and purposes they can trust.